from Your Home and Yard

Object Lessons Series

Bess, C. W., *Children's Object Sermons for the Seasons*, 1026-8
Bess, C. W., *Object-Centered Children's Sermons*, 0734-8
Bess, C. W., *Sparkling Object Sermons for Children*, 0824-7
Bess, C. W., & Roy DeBrand, *Bible-Centered Object Sermons for Children*, 0886-7
Biller, Tom & Martie, *Simple Object Lessons for Children*, 0793-3
Bruinsma, Sheryl, *Easy-to-Use Object Lessons*, 0832-8
Bruinsma, Sheryl, *More Object Lessons for Very Young Children*, 1075-6
Bruinsma, Sheryl, *New Object Lessons*, 0775-5
Bruinsma, Sheryl, *Object Lessons for Every Occasion*, 0994-4
Bruinsma, Sheryl, *Object Lessons for Special Days*, 0920-0
Bruinsma, Sheryl, *Object Lessons for Very Young Children*, 0956-1
Claassen, David, *Object Lessons for a Year*, 2514-1
Connelly, H. W., *47 Object Lessons for Youth Programs*, 2314-9
Coombs, Robert, *Concise Object Sermons for Children*, 2541-9
Coombs, Robert, *Enlightening Object Lessons for Children*, 2567-2
Cooper, Charlotte, *50 Object Stories for Children*, 2523-0
Cross, Luther, *Easy Object Stories*, 2502-8
Cross, Luther, *Object Lessons for Children*, 2315-7
Cross, Luther, *Story Sermons for Children*, 2328-9
De Jonge, Joanne, *More Object Lessons from Nature*, 3004-8
De Jonge, Joanne, *Object Lessons from Nature*, 2989-9
Edstrom, Lois, *Contemporary Object Lessons for Children's Church*, 3432-9
Gebhardt, Richard, & Mark Armstrong, *Object Lessons from Science Experiments*, 3811-1
Godsey, Kyle, *Object Lessons About God*, 3841-3
Hendricks, William, *Object Lessons Based on Bible Characters*, 4373-5
Hendricks, William, & Merle Den Bleyker, *Object Lessons from Sports and Games*, 4134-1
Hendricks, William, & Merle Den Bleyker, *Object Lessons That Teach Bible Truths*, 4172-4
Loeks, Mary, *Object Lessons for Children's Worship*, 5584-9
McDonald, Roderick, *Successful Object Sermons*, 6270-5
Runk, Wesley, *Object Lessons from the Bible*, 7698-6
Squyres, Greg, *Simple Object Lessons for Young Children*, 8330-3
Sullivan, Jessie, *Object Lessons and Stories for Children's Church*, 8037-1
Sullivan, Jessie, *Object Lessons with Easy-to-Find Objects*, 8190-4
Trull, Joe, *40 Object Sermons for Children*, 8831-3

Object Lessons
from Your Home and Yard

Joanne E. De Jonge

Baker Books
A Division of Baker Book House Co
Grand Rapids, Michigan 49516

Published by Baker Books
a division of Baker Book House Company
P.O. Box 6287, Grand Rapids, MI 49516–6287

ISBN 0–8010–3026–9

Printed in the United States of America

This book is dedicated to
JESUS
who loves little children.

Contents

Introduction

This book is for the rank beginner, the "old hand," and anyone between.

If you are a rank beginner, you can use any lesson exactly as it stands. The tone is conversational and the words are simple. Appropriate gestures are suggested within parentheses. Follow each lesson exactly as it is written and you will present an object lesson that young children will understand and remember.

If you are an "old hand" at this and already keep kids spellbound with your lessons, you can use this book for ideas. Every concept in this book is paired with an appropriate and very common object. Some difficult concepts are approached at a slightly different angle from what may have occurred to you. Use the language with which you are comfortable, ignore the "stage directions," and use this book to spark your imagination.

If you have absolutely no time available and cannot even rustle through your closets for an object, check the first seven lessons. You and the children are walking objects; each of the first lessons calls for nothing more. Yet each is a solid lesson with a reminder—an object—which the children certainly will carry with them throughout the week.

If you are superorganized and have plenty of time, peruse this book for lessons you would like to use. Some lessons have optional parts, which you may choose or ignore, depending on your situation. Some give a choice of objects. You may have to buy a few objects, such as red construction paper or a plant bulb. Two or three of these lessons require some preparation, such as positioning or parching a house-plant for a while. Most of these objects are absolutely common, and none of the preparations require inordinate amounts of time.

If you are a young person in charge of devotions at school or for a youth group, use this book for ideas. How many other young people have given devotions with a visual aid? With this book, you can lead devotions that your peers won't forget.

If you are not in charge of devotions, or object lessons, or anything else like that—if you are an adult who thinks object lessons are only for children—read through this book anyway. I have found that simplifying a difficult concept to a form that children can understand often helps clarify that concept for adults. It is refreshing to approach Scripture as a little child.

I have been particularly blessed in the writing of this book. It is my prayer that you and many children will be blessed by its use.

Elephant Tails and Adult Knees

For the rank beginner and anyone else who would like to review.

Before you get all tied up into what object you're going to use, exactly what words you'll say, how much time you'll take, and how in the world you're going to do this, it's good to mentally back up and look at the overall picture. When you have the general form of a lesson in mind and know a few basics of the delivery, those less important details will fall into place. Then you can concentrate on the concept, the eternal truth you are trying to teach.

The general form of an object lesson usually falls into three tried-and-true parts: (1) capturing the children's attention with an object, (2) using that tangible object to teach an intangible truth, and (3) in review, connecting the object and the truth so that children will recall the truth when they see the object.

An object lesson is not a Bible story. It is a lesson from which the children learn one kernel of truth. Keeping the form in mind helps you to avoid a rambling lesson or story.

It also may help you remember what you are going to say. If you are comfortable speaking in your own words, you only need remember that kernel of truth and how you are going to link it to the object.

Language, of course, should be simple enough so that the youngest child present can understand every word you say. If you are stuck on a big word, acknowledge that it's a big word and explain it. If you are not familiar with a child's vocabulary, you may want to practice. A few minutes of practice (or even looking up a synonym) is better than fumbling around looking for a definition during the delivery.

It only makes sense that the object should be one that is common to the children. If the lesson is beautifully constructed and the children are entranced, but the object is an elephant's tail, the children will have nothing to jog their memory during the week. If the object is an apple, chances at recall are much better.

The basics of delivery fall into place when you remember that this is for children, not the adults who may be listening. Often an object lesson is incorporated into a church service. Adults enjoy, remember, and benefit from the object lesson, and can reinforce it at home. It should be done loudly enough for the adults to hear. If they can't see the object, you may want to say what it is for their benefit. Yet you are giving the lesson to the children.

Try to position yourself and the children so that you are facing each other. If children are sitting at your immediate right or left, you will automatically exclude some while you look at others.

Position yourself at eye level with the children. They see enough adult knees whenever the congregation stands in a church service. Physically and symbolically get down to their level no matter what the setting. Sit down with them and look them in the eye. This is your time together.

Keep that bond between you and the children. If they say something outrageous, accept it. If adults laugh, ignore it. If you acknowledge the adults, the bond will shift from you and the children to you and the adults, possibly at the children's expense. For these very few minutes, only the children should exist for you.

Above all, don't worry. If you have prepared ahead of time and have the physical details in hand, worries at this point are probably self-centered. Forget yourself. Concentrate on those precious children and the truth you are to teach them. Trust the Lord to work through you to bless the children—and you.

1

The Doorway to Heaven

Scripture: *I am the gate; whoever enters through me will be saved* (John 10:9).

Concept: Jesus is the only way to heaven.

Object: None. Scout out your sanctuary ahead of time to determine which door you want to use. Make sure it is closed when you begin, so that a child does not wander through it ahead of time.

We're going to take a little walk today, so don't sit down yet. We're going to the pastor's study (or whatever is through the door you have chosen). Are you ready? Let's go.

(Take a few children by the hand and walk with them. It's best if you are in the front lines of the group but not leading follow-the-leader style. Lead the children in the general direction of the room you mentioned but toward the wall in which that door is found. Try to stay quite far from the door. Speak as you walk.) Please stay close to me. There's something I want to show you on the way to the study. We'll do this as a whole group.

(Stop short at the wall.) What is this? This is the way to the pastor's study, but we can't get there. We can't walk through the wall; that's impossible.

We're here and we want to be there, on the other side of this wall. But the wall is in the way. What can we do? *(Pause for response, and repeat the children's responses.)* We can use the door. That's right. That's why the door was put into this wall, to let us into the pastor's study. That's the only way we can get into the study. Let's go.

(Walk over to the door, open it, and let the children in.) There we are. The only way to get in here was through the door. *(If you have time and the layout is right, include the next paragraph. Otherwise, skip to the next one.)*

Now that you're in here, what's the only way out? *(Pause for response.)* Through the door, of course. That's why we have doors, to let us go from one room to another. This door is the only way out.

Let's go back now. *(Lead the children back to their usual object lesson place and have them sit down.)*

Doors and doorways are very important, aren't they? Sometimes we forget how important they are. Did you go through a door to get into church this morning? *(Pause for response.)* Of course you did. What would happen if this church had no doors or doorways? *(Pause for response.)* You wouldn't be able to get inside, would you?

Lots of rooms in this church have only one door. *(If you can see one, use that as an example. Or you can have the children pretend that there is only one door to the sanctuary. Point out that door. Or use the following.)* What about your Sunday school room (or even a bathroom)? There's only one door, and you have to use it to get inside. If that door weren't there, you couldn't get into your Sunday school room.

Did you know that Jesus once called himself a door? Of course, he didn't mean that he was a door like that one. *(Point to a door or doorway.)* Jesus was talking picture language. He meant that he was like a door.

Jesus said that he was the door to heaven. To get to heaven, you have to go through Jesus, just as we had to go through that door to get into the pastor's study. If it weren't for Jesus, it would be as if there were no door to heaven, only walls.

But Jesus came to die for us and make a doorway to heaven. When we believe in Jesus it's like going through Jesus to heaven, just like through a door.

So, when you go to your Sunday school class (or leave church, or go to children's worship), look at all the doorways you go through to get into other rooms. Then think about Jesus, who is the doorway to heaven.

2

God Listens

Scripture: *The eyes of the LORD are on the righteous and his ears are attentive to their cry* (Ps. 34:15).

This is the confidence we have in approaching God: that if we ask anything according to his will, he hears us (1 John 5:14).

Concept: God hears our weakest cries.

Object: None

I want to test your ears today. Nod your head if you can hear me. *(Nod your head to encourage a like response. Speak the next sentence a little more softly.)* Nod your head if you can hear me now. You all have pretty good ears, and you're listening really well. Try this. *(Whisper the next sentence, but loudly enough for the children nearest you to hear.)* Nod your head if you can hear me. *(In a normal tone speak the next sentences.)* Well, some of you heard me. People who are sitting close to me could hear. But you people sitting a little farther away probably couldn't hear me because I was whispering. Let's try one more time. *(This time mouth the words only.)* Raise your hand if you can hear me. *(In a normal tone say the next sentences.)* Nobody heard me that time. I said, "Raise your hand if you can hear me," and nobody raised a hand. I was talking so softly that nobody could have heard me.

Nobody? Isn't there one person who can hear absolutely everything, even things that we say silently? *(Pause for response. If the children don't respond, ask the next question.)* Doesn't God hear our silent prayers? Of course he does. God can hear everything.

Now, pay attention! I want you all to listen really closely. Try as hard as you can to hear me. If you are very quiet and pay attention, I think you'll hear this. *(Wait until the children are quiet and paying attention. Then whisper loudly enough so that every child can hear you.)* God tries to hear you.

Who can tell me what I said? *(Raise your hand as you ask the question to encourage a like response. Call on a child quite far from you.)* Pay attention. Listen closely to what (the child's name) says. He tried to hear me. Let's see what he heard. *(Repeat what the child says. If it was not correct, repeat this paragraph until someone gets it right.)* That's right. I said that God tries to hear you.

You had to pay attention to me to hear me, didn't you? You had to think about me and listen very closely. The Bible says that God listens to us that way. He pays attention to us and listens closely, waiting for us to talk to him. We don't have to shout to get God's attention. He's listening very closely to us already. He hears us, even when we speak silently to him. *(If some of the children misunderstood you when you whispered the last time, you can add, "And you never can speak too quietly for God the way I spoke too quietly for [child's name].)* The Bible says that God is always paying attention to us and he will always hear us.

(You can finish here with the sentences of option 1, or you can add option 2.)

Option 1

Sometimes people whisper too softly for us to hear, don't they? We don't always like that, but our ears are not like God's. We can't hear everything.

But the Bible tells us that God can hear everything. And God is paying attention to you right now, listening to what you have to say to him.

Option 2

I want you to test my ears for a minute. First, everyone together, ask me to stand up (or sit down if you are standing). *(Pause for response, and stand up.)* It's nice to know that you are heard, isn't it? And it's nice that I'll do what you ask.

Now make it a little harder on me. *(Name one child in the back row.)* Talk normally; ask me to stand up. *(Repeat your actions of the previous paragraph.)* That was a little more difficult.

Now, (same child), whisper very softly. *(This time, remain as you are.)* Did I hear (child's name)? *(Pause for response.)* It doesn't seem like it. Maybe I heard

19

but just didn't feel like doing what she asked. I knew what she was asking, didn't I? You don't know if I didn't hear or I just didn't pay any attention.

When we talk to God, we know that he hears and pays attention. The Bible says again and again that God listens to his children, that he pays attention to them, and that he wants them to talk to him, even in whispers. You're never too small or young to talk to God. Right now, he's listening to you.

(Whisper the last lines.) You may go back to your seats. You can even talk to God on the way there. He's listening to you.

3

Guess Who Made You

Scripture: *Know that the Lord is God. It is he who made us, and we are his; we are his people, the sheep of his pasture* (Ps. 100:3).

Concept: God made us and we are his.

Object: None

I didn't bring anything along with me today, because I want you to look at something very special—yourselves! We're going to take a minute to look at our very own bodies.

(Note: Please do everything you tell the children to do.)

Stretch your arm out and look at your hand. Now stretch your fingers apart as far as you can. Now bring your fingers together to make a fist. Now spread your fingers apart again very quickly. Hold still and look at the back of your hand.

Look at your knuckles, the places where your fingers bend. Don't they look a little strange? But all that wrinkled skin is there for a purpose. If it weren't there, you wouldn't be able to bend your fingers. How do your knuckles work? I can't tell you. They must be very complicated, because they let your fingers bend really well.

Who made your knuckles so that they bend so well? *(Pause for response.)* God did, of course. Thank God for your knuckles.

Now turn your hand over and look at your fingertips. Feel your fingertips. Feel down your finger. Feel that bone? Now feel your fingertip again. Feel how soft that is? There's extra padding in your fingertips. When you pick up something, you won't hurt your fingertips.

Now feel the palm of your hand. The skin is rather tough, isn't it? If you were falling and you put out your hands to catch yourself, what would hit the ground first? *(Pause for response.)* Yes, your hands. That's why the skin is so tough—to protect your hands.

Who made your hands with those neat fingertips and tough skin? *(Pause for response.)* That's right, God did. Would you be able to make such neat fingertips? Do you know how to make such tough skin? *(Shake your head as you ask and pause for response.)* Of course not. Only God can do that.

Now, sit very quietly and put your hand over your heart. *(Help the younger children do this.)* Can you feel it beating? Do you know how to make your heart beat? *(Shake your head and pause for response.)* Of course not! Only God knows how to make a beating heart.

Sit even more quietly and try to stop your heart from beating. Think about it very hard. Can you stop your heart? *(Pause for response.)* No! God made our hearts to beat on their own. We don't even have to think about it. Who made your beating heart? *(Pause for response.)* Of course! God did.

Can you wiggle your toes inside your shoes? Now wiggle your feet. Now, bend your knees. Now, sit very quietly again. Who gave you toes to wiggle and feet to shake and knees to bend? *(Pause for response.)* Of course, once more, God did.

Everybody look straight at me. Now everybody turn your heads to one side. Now turn them to the other side. Now look straight at me. Now look at the ceiling. Now look at the floor. What do you turn and bend so you can look all around like that? *(Pause for response.)* Your neck, of course.

Your neck has your throat in it. *(Rub your throat.)* That's a small hard tube. Your neck also has bunches of delicate little nerves in some bumpy bones. *(Rub the back of your neck.)* Yet you can bend and twist your neck without getting the tube and nerves and bones all mixed up.

Could you make such a complicated neck? *(Shake your head and pause for response.)* Of course not. Who gave you such a good neck? *(Pause for response.)* God did! Only God can make a neck like that.

We could go on and on looking at our bodies, but I think you're catching on to my questions. I always ask you who made it. And the answer is always *(pause for response)* God!

Who made us all, inside and out? *(Pause for response.)* God did! So whom do we belong to, inside and out? *(Pause for response.)* That's right! We belong to God.

The Bible says that it is God who has made us and not we ourselves. We are his people. We belong to him.

That's easy to remember, isn't it? Every time you move, you can thank God for your legs or arms or whatever you moved. And when you think about your body, you can remember that God made it, and you belong, body and soul, to him.

4

Hugged by God

Scripture: *The eternal God is your refuge, and underneath are the everlasting arms* (Deut. 33:27).

"Because he loves me," says the LORD, "I will rescue him; I will protect him, for he acknowledges my name. He will call upon me, and I will answer him; I will be with him in trouble, I will deliver him and honor him" (Ps. 91:14–15).

Concept: We are loved and protected within God's arms.

Object: None

Who would like a hug today? *(Pause for response and hug as many of the children as possible. If they are shy, ask the next question. If many children want hugs, continue to speak [substituting hugs for other gestures] as you hug them.)*

How many of you like to sit on Mom's or Dad's lap (or the lap of an adult who cares about you) and have them hug you? *(Raise your hand as you ask the question to encourage a like response.)* I think that everyone likes a hug now and then. Even grownups like hugs. A hug makes you feel loved and protected.

When you fall and hurt yourself a little, does a hug seem to help the hurt go away? *(Nod as you ask and pause for response.)* Sure! At least it makes you feel better, doesn't it?

If someone is mean to you and makes you want to cry, does a hug help? *(Nod and pause for response.)* Of course! A hug tells you that someone loves you.

Pretend for a minute that a big bully is after you. Would you feel safe if you were in Dad's or Mom's arms? *(Nod and pause for response.)*

There's something about a hug—being in someone's big, strong arms—that makes us feel safe and loved.

But we can't always be hugged, can we? Can you ride your bicycle while someone is hugging you? *(Pause for response.)* Can someone make dinner while you're sitting on their lap and they're hugging you? *(Pause for response.)* No. Sometimes the hug has to stop, although we know that we are loved. Can I hug all of you at once? *(Pause for response.)* Of course not! I'm not big enough to hug all of you at the same time, so we get our hugs one at a time.

There is someone who is big enough to hug all of us at the same time. And he's big enough to hug us all of the time, no matter what we're doing. Who is that? *(Pause for response.)* Of course, God!

God said that he will always be a safe place for us. He said that if we love him he will protect us, be with us in trouble, and answer whenever we call on him. He even said that his arms would be underneath us. That's like a giant hug, isn't it?

Does God really have arms like ours? *(Shake your head as you ask, and pause for response.)* No! God doesn't have a body like we do. God is much too big and great for that. But he did say that he loves us, that he will be with us and protect us. And then, so that we could understand, he said that his arms are underneath us. God is always hugging us in love.

You may go back to your seats now. And you may want to collect a hug when you get there. That can help you to remember that, even when a hug from Mom or Dad ends, God keeps hugging you close to him, forever.

5

Hold That Tongue!

Scripture: *With the tongue we praise our Lord and Father, and with it we curse men, who have been made in God's likeness. Out of the same mouth come praise and cursing. My brothers, this should not be* (James 3:9–10).

Concept: Each of us should learn to control what we say.

Object: None but the children's tongues

I didn't bring anything along with me today, because I knew that each of you would come here with what we need. We're going to think about our tongues for a little while.

Can you stick out your tongue? *(Stick your tongue out to demonstrate and frown while you do it.)* It's usually not nice to stick out our tongues, is it? So let's put them back.

Now let's try something a little nicer. Can you pretend that you just had a delicious ice cream cone and are licking your lips? Ummm! *(Lick your lips with a big smile on your face to demonstrate.)* That's better.

Did you notice something? We can do not-so-nice things *(stick out your tongue)* and nice things *(lick your lips)* all with the same tongue.

Sometimes we cannot completely control our tongues. Try this. Say "black bug's blood" three times really fast without getting mixed up. *(Pause while the children try it.)* It's hard to control your tongue there, isn't it?

Now try this. *(Stick your tongue out of your mouth with the sides curled. Pause while the children try it.)* Almost everyone can do that.

Can you stick out your tongue and curl the tip up? *(If you can do this, demonstrate. Pause while they try it.)* Not many people can do that.

So, what have we learned? We can do nice things and not-so-nice things with our tongues. And we can't always completely control our tongues.

Now let's try something else. Can you say "God loves you" without using your tongue? *(Demonstrate by sticking your tongue out of your mouth so the children can see you're not using it.)* You really can't say anything without using your tongue, but try anyway. *(Pause while they try. Note: Some more vocal children will probably say that they can talk without using their tongues, so don't pause too long.)*

Now, use your tongue, and say very clearly, "God loves you." *(Pause while the children say it.)* That's great! You really need your tongue to talk, don't you?

You can use your tongue to say both good and bad things. I'm going to give you a choice. You may say either "God loves you"or "I hate you" in the next few seconds. Either "God loves you" or "I hate you." Say it softly. Go. *(Pause, while they speak.)*

I'm not going to ask you what you said. But I am going to ask you, who controlled what you said? Who decided exactly what you would say, you or me? *(Pause for response.)* You did, of course. You alone can decide exactly how you're going to use your tongue.

The Bible talks about how you use your tongue. It says that out of the same mouth come praise and cursing. That means you can say "God loves you," and you can say "I hate you" with the same tongue. But the Bible says that shouldn't be. We should learn to control our tongues.

Of course, there are some ways we can't control our tongues. Not everyone can do this *(demonstrate a "side roll")* or this *(demonstrate [or try to] a "curl tip").* But we can control our tongues in other ways. And especially in speaking, God wants us to control what we say, to say only good things.

So, before we finish, let's practice controlling what we say. Let's try saying some good things together. How about "God loves you"? *(Pause while the children respond.)* Or "I love Jesus." *(Pause while they respond. Add whatever phrases you would like to add.)*

Now I think we're in good practice. Each of us can remember to hold our tongue and control what we say.

Peek-a-Boo with God

Scripture: *But the eyes of the Lord are on those who fear him* (Ps. 33:18).

"Can anyone hide in secret places so that I cannot see him?" declares the Lord. "Do not I fill heaven and earth?" declares the Lord (Jer. 23:24).

Concept: God is always watching over us.

Object: None

How many of you have played this little game? Watch me. *(Cover your eyes with your hands, then quickly pull them away.)* Peek-a-boo, I see you! *(Do it again.)*

That's a simple little game, isn't it? How many of you have done that? *(Raise your hand to encourage a like response and pause slightly.)* We probably all have done it at some time. Or people have done that to us when we were very young. Adults like to play peek-a-boo with babies. You may have done it with a younger brother or sister.

The idea is that you can't see another person like this. *(Cover your eyes.)* But then, suddenly, you can again. *(Pull your hands away.)* Peek-a-boo! That makes little children laugh.

They like to be watched, so they like this part. *(Cover your eyes, but then quickly pull your hands off.)* They'll laugh when you look at them. Usually they're very quiet during this part. *(Cover your eyes for a long second.)* Pull your hands off and look at them *(do it)* and they'll laugh. You're watching them again. They like it when you watch them.

Sometimes you can do it this way. *(Hide yourself behind the pulpit. Speak from behind there.)* You disappear, and they think that they're hidden from you. Then you pop out, *(do it)* peek-a-boo! and they laugh.

I think you could go far away from home and play this peek-a-boo *(hands over your eyes, then quickly uncovered)* and anyone would recognize it. Everyone plays peek-a-boo at some time.

Well, not everyone. God doesn't play peek-a-boo. He never hides his eyes *(put your hands over your eyes)* from us. And he's never away from us. *(Indicate the pulpit where you hid, or go back and hide briefly.)*

The Bible says that the eyes of the Lord are on those who fear him, which means those who know they are loved by him. It doesn't say once in a while. It doesn't say most of the time. It simply says that the eyes of the Lord are on his children. If you love God, he is always watching over you.

And you can't go anyplace where God can't see you. The Bible says that he fills heaven and earth. God is here. He's at your house to take care of you.

He's in your secret hiding place to hear you talk or pray to him. God is everywhere. So, wherever you go, God sees you and always watches over you.

Do you know what's so good about that? God loves you! So he's watching over you in love. He's not spying on you. He knows what you do and say anyway. But his eyes are always on you. He's always watching over you because he loves you. He always wants to see you so he can take care of you.

This is really a simple little game. *(Play peek-a-boo once.)* You've probably outgrown it by now. But you can play it with a younger brother or sister or neighbor.

You can even change it a bit. Try this. *(Play peek-a-boo two times.)* Peek-a-boo, God sees you! Peek-a-boo, God loves you!

That little game can help you remember that God never plays peek-a-boo and will never leave you. He is always watching over you and taking care of you.

Don't Bother Me

Scripture: *The LORD is compassionate and gracious, slow to anger, abounding in love. . . . But from everlasting to everlasting the LORD's love is with those who fear him* (Ps. 103:8, 17).

Concept: God is never too busy to be bothered.

Object: None. Prompt one of the older children before the lesson to ask you a question (loudly) two times. Warn the child about how you will answer.

(When the children come up and settle themselves, keep yourself busy with something. Fuss with your clothes or the microphone or page through your Bible. If you usually help the children get settled, help them but with a bit of impatience. Then begin your fussing. When the prompted child asks the question, answer without looking up.)

What if I paid no attention to you? How would you feel if I said, "Don't bother me! Can't you see I'm busy?"

(Look over the children and change your expression to a bright smile.) You wouldn't feel very good, would

you? I told (the prompted child's name) to ask me a question and warned him that I was going to be crabby, busy with something else.

Did it make you feel bad to hear me sound so crabby? *(Nod your head and pause for response.)* Sure! No one likes to hear, "Don't bother me!" Yet, we all hear it once in a while.

Does your mom or dad ever say that to you? *(Nod and pause for response.)* Probably. No adult is always completely patient with kids.

Sometimes, when you bother Dad or Mom again and again for something, do they become angry with you? *(Nod and pause for response.)* Or, sometimes, if they're really busy and you interrupt, do they say, "Don't bother me, I'm busy"? *(Nod and pause for response.)* Sometimes, maybe just once in a while, do they say, "Don't bother me," when you really do have to talk to them? *(Nod and pause for response.)* Probably everybody does that sometimes. Your parents may sometimes really be too busy to listen to you. Or, they may just be having a bad day, and they're out of patience. They can't be bothered right then. They're not perfect. Everybody has crabby times for no good reason. Nobody's perfect.

Nobody, except God. God is perfect. And, do you know what? God never has crabby times for no reason at all. God never has a time that he can't be bothered. And God never says, "Don't bother me, I'm busy."

The Bible tells us that God is compassionate, slow to anger, and abounding in love. That means that

God loves us very much, he doesn't want us ever to feel bad or hurt inside, and he's got lots and lots of patience. God is never too busy to listen to you when you talk to him. You are always the most important thing in the world to God when you talk to him. He never, ever feels bothered by his children talking to him. You love him, and he will always love you. And he will always, always have time to listen to you.

Your parents try to be very patient with you, too. But, sometimes they are very busy, and they are not perfect. So, the next time Dad or Mom says to you, *(frown and say snappishly)* "Don't bother me, I'm busy," be patient with them. Wait just a little while. And remember that God is very, very patient and is never too busy to listen to you, his child.

Glued to God's Love

Scripture: *For I am convinced that neither death nor life, neither angels nor demons, neither the present nor the future, nor any powers, neither height nor depth, nor anything else in all creation, will be able to separate us from the love of God that is in Christ Jesus our Lord* (Rom. 8:38–39).

Concept: Nothing can separate us from God's love.

Objects: Glue (the most common glue in your area in a container that the children will easily recognize, such as a yellow gluestick or Elmer's), two pieces of paper of different size and color glued tightly together.

Who can tell me what this is? *(Hold up the glue and pause for response.)* Yes, it's glue—common glue that we use to glue two pieces of paper together. You smear the glue on one piece of paper *(mimic gluing papers together)*, put the other piece on top, and wait for the glue to dry. The papers are stuck together for good.

I already glued two pieces of paper together to show you how strong the glue is. *(Hold up the paper.)*

Can you see the small blue (or whatever color) paper glued to the larger white one? The glue is dry, and the papers are stuck together.

I can't shake them apart. *(Shake the papers.)* I can't pull them apart. *(Gently mimic pulling one paper off the other.)* I can't poke them apart. *(Probe with a finger between the two papers.)* There's no way I'm going to get these papers apart. The blue one is stuck on the white one for good.

You've probably used glue like this in Sunday school or children's worship or school. How many of you have glued papers together? *(Raise your hand as you ask the question to encourage a like response.)* Good. Then you know what I'm talking about. You know how tightly these papers are glued together. *(Shake the papers once more.)* You know they won't come apart.

That's how tightly you are glued to God's love. In fact, you're glued more tightly than that. *(Pause for effect.)* That sounds really strange, doesn't it? Glued to God's love. But it's not strange at all.

The Bible says that nothing in the whole world is going to separate you from God's love. You are stuck together, glued to God's love forever. *(Shake the papers.)* The strongest person in the world can't pull you away from God's love. *(Mimic pulling one paper off the other.)* Something that happens someday in the future can't separate you from God's love. *(Probe with a finger between the two papers.)* Absolutely nothing in all creation can separate you from God's love.

(Hold up the papers.) You are glued to God's love forever and ever.

God loves you and isn't going to let anything come between you and his love. Doesn't that make you feel very safe?

This glue *(hold up the glue container)* works best on paper. It doesn't always work perfectly on other things. But God's glue works perfectly. Nothing is ever going to separate you from his love.

Planting Gardens

9

Scripture: *Remember this: Whoever sows sparingly will also reap sparingly, and whoever sows generously will also reap generously* (2 Cor. 9:6).

Concept: You reap what you sow.

Objects: Packets of seeds, preferably with pictures on them. (This can also be done with various seeds, not in packets. This can be done as well with flower seeds.)

Today I've brought a lot of seeds with me. I'm going to plant a garden soon, and I wanted to show you what I'm going to have in it.

(Hold up a packet so the children can see the picture. Or hold up a handful of seeds and tell, rather than ask, what they are.) What are these? *(Pause for response.)* That's right, they're carrot seeds. Do you like carrots? I'm planting a few rows of these so I can have fresh carrots this summer.

(Hold up another packet.) What about these? Tomatoes! Do you like tomatoes? I think almost everyone does. I'm planting these so that I can have lots of tomatoes next fall.

(Continue in this manner with all the packets or seeds. Involve the children by asking what they are and/or who likes them. Mention with each set of seeds that you are planting those seeds and are going to have and eat and enjoy each crop. If you have time, you can ask the children what they would include in their gardens. What food or flower do they like? That is, what seeds would they plant?)

I picked these seeds with care, because they're all things that I really like. That's why I'm planting these seeds and not some others.

Did you notice that I didn't include any cabbage seeds? I don't care for cabbage, so I left it out of my garden. I also left out eggplant, zucchini, and broccoli *(name a few that you don't care for)*. None of those seeds are going into my garden, because I really don't want any of those vegetables.

(Hold up one of the packets, so the children can see the picture.) Do you think I might get cabbage from these seeds? *(Pause for response.)* Of course not! Unless someone made a mistake, these are carrot seeds, so I'll get carrots.

(Hold up another packet.) Could I possibly get eggplant from these seeds? *(Pause for response.)* No! I'll get tomato plants from tomato seeds.

Whatever seed you plant, that's the kind of vegetable or fruit or flower that grows. That's the way God made the world. Plant a tomato seed and get a tomato plant, not a cabbage. It's very reliable. Whatever we sow, or plant, that's what we'll reap, or pick.

The Bible even says that we reap what we sow. That means, if you plant a certain kind of seed, that's what's going to grow.

But the Bible isn't really talking about planting gardens, is it? The Bible really talks about planting actions. Let me try to explain.

If you are mean to someone, do you think they're going to like you? *(Pause for response.)* Of course not! No one likes people who are mean to them. But if you are nice to someone, then do you think they'll be nice to you? *(Pause for response.)* Probably. You want to be nice to nice people, don't you? Sow kindness, which means to be kind to people, and you reap kindness, which means people will be kind to you.

Try this one. Sow sparingly—in other words, be stingy with your toys, be a selfish person, be grumpy and not loving *(demonstrate with a frown and arms in defensive position)*—and how will people treat you? *(Pause for response.)* That's right, people will probably be grumpy and unloving back. But sow generously—be kind, loving, cheerful, and generous with all you have *(put on a cheerful face with open arms and upraised hands)*—and how will people react? *(Pause for response.)* Yes, they'll usually be kind and loving back to you. Sow sparingly *(frown and defensive posture)* and reap sparingly. Sow generously *(smile and open posture)* and reap generously.

(Show the seed packets once more.) I'm going to sow a garden, and I know exactly what I'll get. But, do you know what? We're all sowing gardens right now. Sow generously *(cheerful and open)*, sow seeds of love, and you will reap generously, too.

10

Play Ball!

Scripture: *It was he who gave some to be apostles, some to be prophets, some to be evangelists, and some to be pastors and teachers, to prepare God's people for works of service, so that the body of Christ may be built up* (Eph. 4:11–12).

Concept: We each have our own talent to use for God. Everyone's talent and its use is important.

Objects: Several different kinds of balls. Those used here are a golf ball, a tennis ball, and a football.

I brought some balls with me today. They're all different, because they're all used a little differently. Maybe you can help me sort them out. *(Dump all the balls into one pile.)*

(Hold up the golf ball.) What kind of ball is this? *(Pause for response.)* Yes, it's a golf ball. People use it when they play golf. It's a small, hard ball, perfect for playing golf.

(Hold up the tennis ball.) What is this ball called? *(Pause for response.)* Yes, it's a tennis ball. People use a

tennis racket to hit this over a net to each other. This is softer than a golf ball and it bounces quite well. *(Bounce the ball.)* Some people play with this in other ways besides tennis. Maybe you just want to bounce this ball. *(Bounce it again.)* It could be a good ball for playing catch. *(Throw it to one of the children.)* It's soft, so it won't hurt you. Although this is a tennis ball, it has several uses.

But it's not good for everything. Could someone play golf with a tennis ball? *(Shake your head and pause for response.)* Probably not. This ball isn't as heavy as a golf ball, and it's too big. This would probably go flying all over the golf course.

But then, could you play tennis with this golf ball? *(Show the golf ball, shake your head, and pause for response.)* No! This golf ball is too small and heavy. It might ruin a tennis racket. Would you like to play catch with this golf ball? *(Pretend that you are going to throw it to someone.)* No! This ball is too hard. It might hurt you if you didn't catch it right.

We'll use the tennis ball *(indicate the tennis ball)* for tennis and playing catch. We'll use the golf ball for golf.

Here's another ball. *(Hold up the football.)* What do you play with this ball? *(Pause for response.)* That's right, you play football with it.

Could you play tennis with this ball? *(Pause for response.)* No! Could you play golf with it? *(Pause for response.)* Of course not.

(Show the golf ball.) Would you play football with this? *(Pause for response.)* No! *(Show the tennis ball.)* Would you play football with this? *(Pause for response.)* That would be difficult, wouldn't it? You play football with this football. *(Indicate the football.)*

(If you have brought more balls, continue in this manner. Ask the children how the ball is used. Then ask if it can be used for another purpose, for which it obviously cannot be. Point out the ball perfect for the purpose you mention. Point out that each ball has an important purpose, but no ball can fit all purposes.)

(Hold up all the balls.) Which, of all these balls, do you think, is most important? Is it the golf ball? *(Indicate each ball as you mention it, and pause for a mixed response.)* Certainly, we can't play golf very well without this ball. Yet, what about this tennis ball? It's very important when we play tennis, and we can use it for catch. Of course, this football is important, too. You can't play football without it. You can't use it for much else, but you certainly need it for a game of football.

Each of these balls is important, isn't it? None is really more important than the other. Each was made for a certain game. If you want to play that game, you need that ball. Each ball is different from any other ball, and each ball is important.

Did you know that's what God says about us? You're not a golf ball, of course, or a tennis ball or a football. But, in a way, all of us together are like a whole bunch of different balls.

God says that he made each one of us to be different. He gave each of us different talents and abilities to work for him. No one is more important than anyone else. All of us are important in our own ways. Each of us should use what God gave us.

Do you sing well? Maybe that's your talent to use. Are you naturally very friendly? You can use that by welcoming new people to church. Do you draw well? Perhaps someday you'll be a Christian artist. Or maybe you're good at cheering up sick people. At any rate, God gave each of us some ability, some talent, something to do for him.

(Hold up the balls, all together.) Just like these balls, each of us is different. Is one more important than the other? *(Pause for response.)* Of course not! Each of you is made by God to be his child in a special way. God can use each of you. And each of you is important in your own way.

11

Don't Forget the Salt

Scripture: *You are the salt of the earth* (Matt. 5:13).

Concept: Christians should make their influence felt.

Object: A bag of unsalted, unbuttered popcorn, enough for each child to have two handfuls; a salt shaker

I popped some popcorn last night so you could chew on it a bit while we're talking. Please just take one little handful. *(Pass out the popcorn. Continue to speak as you pass it.)* Please don't eat it right away. Wait until everyone has some. There's not very much, just enough for each of us to have a little taste. We'll be careful not to spill it on the carpet. Does everyone have some? OK, you may eat some of it now, but keep a little in your hand.

(Take some popcorn yourself and eat it.) Ugh, this doesn't taste very good. There's something missing. What is it? *(Pause for response.)* That's right, there's no salt on this popcorn.

I didn't really forget the salt. I left it off on purpose, because I wanted you to taste how strange it is without salt. In fact, I left the butter off, too, because butter has a little salt in it. A little salt goes a long way. A little salt does a lot. This would taste a lot better with salt, wouldn't it?

What other food tastes better with salt than without? Can you think of any? *(Pause for response. If no response is forthcoming, give the children some ideas: eggs, potato chips, pretzels, potatoes, meat, vegetables.)* In fact, we put salt on just about everything we eat, don't we? If you don't salt your food at the table, someone probably shakes a little salt into it when the food is cooking. Our food would taste a lot different if we didn't have salt. Salt is very important.

Maybe that's why Jesus called us salt. He did, you know. He said that we are the salt of the earth, and that's very important.

Now you can eat the rest of your popcorn. When you chew on it, think of how blah it tastes. Not much to it. That's the way the world is without Christians.

Jesus wants us to make the world better for him, sort of like the way we make popcorn taste better with salt. What can we do to salt the world to make it better for Jesus?

Are there things we can say? *(Pause for response. Repeat each response, shaking some salt into the bag as you do. Suggestions follow in case there is no response.)* We can talk about Jesus, can't we? On Christmas we can talk about Jesus' birthday, which is much more important than Santa Claus. Whenever we have a chance we can tell people about Jesus. That's salting the world for Jesus.

Are there things we can do? *(Proceed as you did above.)* How about being kind to people? *(Continue shaking salt into the bag at each sentence.)* Didn't Jesus say that we should do to others as we want others to do to us? Didn't Jesus tell us to love one another? Didn't Jesus tell us to be kind to our enemies? Aren't we supposed to love and honor our parents? When we do those things, we are salting the world for Jesus.

Now I think I've got enough salt on this popcorn. And you probably have some more ideas about how you can be salt for Jesus.

On your way back to your seats you may each take a few kernels of this popcorn with salt. Hold them until you get back to your seat. Try not to drop them. Then, eat one kernel at a time. With each kernel, try to think of another way you can salt the world for Jesus.

You are the salt of the earth. Don't forget that you are salt. It makes a big difference for Jesus.

12

God's Puppets

Scripture: *I no longer live, but Christ lives in me* (Gal. 2:20).

Concept: We should let Jesus Christ control our lives.

Object: A hand puppet

(Have your puppet ready to go, so that the first words out of your mouth are from the puppet.)

Good morning, boys and girls. I'm so happy to see you. My name is Isabel, and I'm a dragon (or whatever kind of puppet you have.). But I'm a nice dragon because (your own name) is a nice person. *(Let the puppet look at you.)* And, of course, (your own name) is making me look alive. But enough of that.

How are all of you? Are you fine? *(Nod the puppet's head and pause for response.)* Good! It's a beautiful morning, isn't it? *(Nod it again and pause for response.)* It's such a nice warm spring (or whatever) day. I think I'll go huff around the woods this afternoon. I'll make it a picnic. You are such nice children, someday I would like you to have a picnic with me.

Would you like that? *(Nod the puppet and wait for response.)*

(Note: The above paragraph is only a suggestion. What you use depends on the season, your church, and your children. The idea is for the puppet to first acknowledge that it is not acting on its own, then to establish a bond between the puppet and the children.)

(Take the puppet off your hand and speak directly to the children.) I know I didn't have any of you fooled. You all knew that was a puppet. It even *said* it was a puppet. But it still was kind of nice, wasn't it?

Was that a nice or a mean puppet? *(Pause for response.)* It was a nice puppet, wasn't it? But that's only because I made it nice. I could have made it a mean puppet.

(Put the puppet on and talk through it.) GRRR! *(Snap it at some of the children nearby.)* I'm a big, bad dragon and I don't like you. I'm going to eat you up!

(Take the puppet off.) That was a mean puppet, wasn't it? It was really me being mean through the puppet. After all, I gave the puppet life, didn't I?

(Hold up the limp puppet without your hand in it.) This is just a hunk of material without my hand inside of it. It doesn't do a thing without me. It's really me in it *(put your hand inside)* that gives it life and personality. It's as if I live inside of the puppet. It does nothing on its own. I do what I want to do through the puppet. *(Gesture with the puppet, then take it off.)*

In a very real way, we're all puppets; at least we should be. Who, do you think, should control us? *(Pause for response.)* God! Yes, we know that God wants to control our lives. God wants to live through us.

But we're not absolutely lifeless, are we? *(Hold up the lifeless puppet.)* We control what we say. We can say mean and nasty things, and that's not God talking through us. So we're a little different from this puppet. We have to choose to let God control us. We have to work at it a bit. We have to ask what Jesus wants us to do.

But then you can be God's puppet, can't you? You have the choice of being mean and nasty, or loving and friendly. *(Put the puppet on as you speak.)* How would Jesus act? *(Pause for response.)*

(Next, the puppet speaks.) That's right, girls and boys. Jesus wants us to be loving and friendly. When you do what Jesus wants, you're God's puppet. You're letting Jesus live through you.

(This from you.) You have a choice. You can be selfish and stingy with all your toys, or you can be generous and sharing. How would Jesus be? *(Pause for response.)*

(Next, the puppet speaks.) Yes, I think Jesus would share. So when you're generous and sharing, you're God's puppet. You're letting Jesus live through you.

You get the idea, don't you? Just as we control these little puppets, God wants to control us. Jesus wants to live in us and through us. *(Point to your hand inside the puppet.)* If you think about what Jesus would do and ask him to help you, you can always be God's puppets.

13

Beyond Understanding

Scripture: *"For my thoughts are not your thoughts, neither are your ways my ways,"* declares the LORD. *"As the heavens are higher than the earth, so are my ways higher than your ways and my thoughts than your thoughts"* (Isa. 55:8–9).

Concept: God's thoughts and ways are beyond our understanding.

Object: A worm in a jar (give it a little slightly moist soil); and a sheet of clean, white paper. (*Note*: Any small creature will do. One that will not move fast is preferable. You will have to change your "commands" to suit the creature. You can "try to train" it to go to food or water, turn left or right, start and stop, etc.)

I brought my pet worm with me today. *(Show the children the worm.)* I thought that maybe you could give me some hints on how to train it.

I've been working with it for a few days. I'm trying to teach it to come and to roll over, but it just won't learn. Watch this.

(If you can, arrange the children so that they all can see. Those in the front sit, those behind sit on their knees, and those way in back stand. If you have some children standing, make the next part short. If you have a large number of children, it might be best to do only option 2.)

Option 1

(Gently take or shake the worm out of the jar onto the paper.) I know it can move, so you'd think it could learn to come to me. COME! COME! It doesn't get the idea. Even if I point it toward me *(turn the worm so that it faces you)*, it doesn't come when I call. COME! COME!

Let's try rolling over. I'll show it what to do. ROLL OVER! ROLL OVER! *(As you say that, roll the worm over.)* See if it learned. ROLL OVER! ROLL OVER! ROLL OVER! *(Don't touch the worm this time.)* The thing just won't learn. It understands touching, but it doesn't talk my language. *(Put it back into the jar while the children sit down.)*

Option 2

(Hold the jar up and sideways, so that all can see.) The worm is inside the jar, and I'm trying to get it to crawl toward my tapping. *(Tap on one end of the jar.)* It just doesn't understand. I can drag it, but I can't make it come.

Maybe I can get it to curl itself. *(Take off the lid and say, "CURL! CURL!" into the jar.)* It doesn't do a thing.

(If you can, reach down and curl it while you give the command. Then give the command without touching it.) This worm simply won't learn. It does the right thing when I touch it, so in some way it understands touching. But it doesn't understand my commands.

Continue Lesson

Do you have any ideas on how I can train this worm? *(You can pause for response and repeat the responses, or continue directly.)* I've decided that maybe a worm can't learn things like that.

This worm is created perfectly for its life. But its life usually doesn't include understanding commands like ROLL OVER! It may hear me, but it will never understand. It can't think like we do, can it? It doesn't even know that we're people, or that it's in church. It knows only worm things. People things are beyond its understanding.

In a way, that's how it is with us and God. God doesn't think of us as worms. We're his special creatures, and God loves us. But things that God does and thinks are beyond our understanding. As hard as we try, we can't fully understand God. We know people things. But we're not created to know God things. That's just beyond us.

Sometimes people ask, "Why did God do that?" or "What was God thinking, to do that?" But we can't figure it out, because God is so much greater than we are.

That doesn't mean we can't ever understand God, does it? When God wants us to understand, he talks in people's language. He gave us the Bible. He even sent his son Jesus to live with us! That we can understand. But we'll never understand God completely; he's too great for that.

I'm going to put my worm back where I found it. I'm giving up; I'll never train it. It doesn't understand me, and I don't understand it.

But the neat thing that we can remember is that God understands us. God will never "put us back and give up," because God loves us more than we know. We can't possibly understand all that God does. His thoughts are way beyond ours. But he has told us that he loves us, and we are his special creatures. That, too, is beyond our understanding but the best thing that we can know.

14

Put On a Happy Face!

Scripture: *Rejoice in the Lord always. I will say it again: Rejoice!* (Phil. 4:4).

Concept: Be happy. God loves you!

Object: A happy-face picture, big enough for all the children to see. It would be nice, but not necessary, to have a smaller one for each child.

Who can tell me what this is? *(Hold up the picture. Pause for response.)* That's right, it's a happy face (or smiley face). It makes you feel good just to look at it, doesn't it? *(Pause for response.)*

We used to see lots of happy faces like this one. Some people put happy faces on almost everything. They'd sign their name to a letter and then put a happy face by it. *(Draw a happy face in the air while you say that.)* People put happy faces on their car bumpers. Teachers often drew happy faces on children's papers. *(Draw another happy face in the air.)* Happy faces were all over the place. It was rather nice.

But that was a fad for a while. Some people must have thought that there were too many happy faces. Now there aren't nearly as many *(hold up the happy face picture again)* as there once were. I think it's time to bring happy faces back, don't you? *(Nod as you speak and pause for response.)*

We can start by making *real* happy faces instead of drawing them. What's a happy face, this *(glare or frown at the children)* or this? *(Smile brightly and pause for response.)* Of course, this is. *(Smile brightly again.)* Let's see you put on happy faces. Everybody try a great big smile. *(Look the children over.)* That's great! Those happy faces are better than this! *(Show them the drawn happy face.)*

The Bible tells us always to wear a happy face. It doesn't actually say, "Wear a happy face always," but it does say, "Rejoice in the Lord always." To rejoice means to be happy. And when you're really happy, you'll have a happy face.

What else do you do when you're really happy? *(Pause for response. If it isn't forthcoming, prompt the children with the following questions.)* Do you sometimes sing when you're happy? Do you sometimes dance when you're happy? Are you usually cheerful when you're happy? Sure! You can sing, dance, and be cheerful—all with a happy face when you rejoice in the Lord.

Do you know why we can wear such happy faces, why we can really be happy? *(Pause only slightly.)* Because Jesus loves us! He said that he loves you and you and you *(point at individuals)*, and that he loves me. We are God's children because Jesus loves us. There's nothing to be scared of or sad about. Jesus loves us and that's what counts. We can always, always rejoice, or be happy in the Lord. And we can show it with our happy faces.

Some of us have forgotten already. Let's try those happy faces one more time. *(Pause and look them over.)* That's wonderful! *(Make sure you are smiling.)* Rejoice in the Lord, and put on a happy face.

(If you have a happy face for each child, include this paragraph.) Now, just so you don't forget about your happy face this week, I've got one for each of you. Take it home and put it where you'll see it every day. That can remind you to smile, because God loves you!

15

Smooth Stones
from Rough Edges

Scripture: *Not only so, but we also rejoice in our sufferings, because we know that suffering produces perseverance; perseverance, character; and character, hope* (Rom. 5:3–4).

Concept: Rough times can make us better Christians.

Objects: One rough stone and one smooth stone. (*Note:* This works very well with a smooth stone for each child. You can get these at a beach, a landscaping nursery, or a hobby store.)

I picked up this stone the other day *(show the rough stone)* and was going to keep it. But now I think it may be too rough. Look at the jagged edges. I don't want that in my pocket (or on my desk).

I kept this just long enough to show you the difference between it and this. *(Show the smooth stone.)* This is so much smoother. It feels nice in my hand. It will go well in my pocket (or on my desk).

(If you have enough smooth stones for everyone, pass them out now. As you pass them, tell the children to rub

them between their hands, feel the smooth edges, and then keep them safe in one fist.)

This stone (or these) hasn't always been as smooth as it is now. *(Rub it between your fingers.)* Most stones, when they break off from big rocks, are rough and jagged, like this. *(Indicate the rough stone.)* The difference now is that this one *(indicate the smooth stone)* has been knocked around a bit.

(Use all or some of the following sentences. Gesture appropriately, so that the children can imagine rocks tumbling, washing, etc.) This probably spent some time in a lake or ocean. Waves pushed it here and there. It probably bumped against a lot of other stones. And sand washed over it. It may have spent some time on a windy beach. Sand blew against it all the time, pick, pick, picking away at the rough edges. Maybe someone who hauls rocks around put it in a big truck with lots of other stones. And they crashed and banged against each other. It could have even spent some time in a rock polisher, a machine that tumbles rocks on purpose.

All that tumbling, banging around, and wind and water gradually wore the rough edges away from this stone (or your stones). Now it's nice and smooth. It's gone through a lot to wear off its rough edges and become this smooth.

In a way, you could almost say that people are like these stones. People go through a lot sometimes, too. They're banged around in life. *(During these next sentences, make the same gestures that you did for the rocks tumbling, washing, etc.)* Your best friend moves away. Somebody takes your favorite toy. You're not doing well in school but trying really hard. Someone teases you for no reason at all. *(Here's a good opportunity to slip in some hard knocks some of the children have had, if you know them: death, a divorce, etc. Don't mention by name or call attention to the child. Just slip in a little reference so that only that child knows what you are talking about.)*

You know, things like that happen to grownups, too. And they wonder, just as kids do, why some things happen. Why is life bumpy at times? Why do these bad things happen?

God doesn't tell us exactly why he lets certain things happen. But God did say that suffering produces character. In other words, these things that happen can make us better Christians.

When your friend moves away, maybe you find new friends and keep the old. If someone takes your toy, you know how it feels to be without and you learn to share. When you really try in school, you learn a lot of patience. And, if someone teases you for no reason, you learn how to be gentle with people, don't you?

That's like becoming a smooth stone. *(Hold up the smooth stone. If each child has one, ask the children to feel them now.)* The rough edges are off. God is shaping you the way he wants you to be. Just as the wind and waves made this a smooth stone, all those little bumps in life will make you a better Christian.

(If the children have stones you can add this.) Take your smooth stone home. You can even keep it in your pocket. Then, when you hit a rough time, feel that smooth stone. And remember that God is helping you become a better Christian.

16

Plug into the Power

Scripture: *Finally, be strong in the Lord and in his mighty power* (Eph. 6:10).

Concept: Our strength comes from God.

Objects: A hair dryer, a small radio, and a Bible. (This can be done with any small appliances. If you use a radio, check ahead of time to be sure you can get reception inside the building. You must have access to an electrical outlet for this lesson. Find the outlet in advance, and arrange the children so that your access to it is easy.)

Something is wrong with this hair dryer. *(Show the unplugged dryer.)* It won't work. *(Flip the on-off switch a few times.)* It must be broken. Does anyone have an idea of what's wrong? *(Pause for response. If the children don't tell you to plug it in, show them the plug and ask again.)*

It's simple. I forgot to plug it in! *(Plug the dryer in and turn it on.)* There, now it works. It only had to be plugged into the power.

I'll bet that's what's wrong with this radio, too. It didn't make a sound this morning, didn't do me a bit of good. *(Turn the radio on without plugging it in. Make sure that you don't leave the volume too high.)* Should I try plugging this in, too? Maybe it will work then. *(Plug the radio in.)*

There we go. This radio doesn't work at all until it's plugged in. Unplug it, and it will stop. *(Unplug the radio.)* It loses all power.

What's the source of power for this radio and this dryer? What makes these work well? *(Pause for response. How you answer depends on the children's response.)* That's right, you have to plug it in. Does the power come from that little gadget in the wall? Sort of, but it's not really that outlet that does the work. There are wires behind it. What's in those wires? (Or, There's electricity in those wires.)

This dryer and radio are both electrical gadgets. They are made to work with electricity. If we don't plug them into the electricity, they don't work at all.

I don't really understand electricity. That's too complicated for me. All I understand is that I must plug these in. The power is there, waiting for me to use it. *(Plug the radio in.)* I plug in, and I've got the power.

We can't plug ourselves into this power, can we? *(Put your finger near the socket.)* In fact, doing this *(finger near socket)* can be very dangerous. Only these electrical appliances *(indicate)* use this power.

But we have a much better power. It's power to keep us going our whole lives. It makes us good strong Christians. This power is always nearby; we only have to plug into it. Who is this power? *(Pause for response. If the children don't respond, ask "Who gives us life?")* That's right, God is our power.

We have to plug into our power, just like we plug in this radio. We can go from day to day and try not to think about God, but then he won't give us power to be good Christians. We have to plug in to really get the full power.

How can we plug into God, our power? *(Hold up one of the plugs and pause for response. If it is not forthcoming, give a hint by assuming an attitude of prayer.)* That's right, we can pray every day. We can ask God for power to help us be good Christians.

How else can we plug into this power? *(Hold up a plug, show the Bible, and pause for response.)* Yes, we can read the Bible, or we can listen while someone else reads the Bible to us. That way we can know how God wants us to live. And by his power, we can live just as he wants us to.

(Show the "dead" dryer and radio.) Just as these gadgets are "dead," no good without their power *(indicate the outlet)*, so Christians are "dead," not good without God's power. *(Indicate the Bible.)*

So, the next time you turn on a radio or a hair dryer, think about the power that keeps it going. Then plug into your power; say a little prayer that God will help you be his loving and obedient child.

17

Imitating God

Scripture: *Be imitators of God, therefore, as dearly loved children* (Eph. 5:1).

Concept: We should try to imitate Jesus in our lives.

Objects: A toy saw and hammer, toy pots and pans, and a toy iron. (You can use any toys that imitate adults' equipment.)

Here's a toy saw and hammer. (*Hold up the saw and hammer.*) How many of you have played with something like this? (*Pause for response.*) Who knows how to play with this? (*Pause for response.*) I'll do it as you tell me what to do. We'll just pretend we have some wood. Shall I saw the board first, or should I nail it into place and then cut it? (*Pause for response.*) I guess I'd better saw it first. (*Pretend to saw.*) There, now it's the right size. I should nail it right here. (*Indicate a place on the floor.*) How do I use the hammer? Do I hold this end (*indicate the wrong end*) and pound with the handle? No? Do I hold it like this? (*Hold the handle.*) Yes? Now I can pound like this? (*Pretend to drive a nail into the wood.*)

You know quite a bit about this. You must have seen someone do this, or maybe you had a chance to play with these tools yourself.

Here's another toy, a small thing like one that grownups have. *(Show the pots and pans.)* I'm going to play that I'm boiling water. *(Pretend to fill a pan with water, put it on a stove, and turn on the heat.)* There, it's boiling. *(Take the pan off the "stove.")* Shall I pour it into my lap? *(Pause for response.)* Of course, we're only pretending, but you know how to use these, don't you?

One more toy. *(Show the iron.)* I'll plug it in *(pretend to plug it in)* to iron some clothes. How many of you know how to play with this iron? *(Pause for response.)* Probably most of you do, right?

You know how to play with these toys because you've seen grownups use the real things. When you play, you copy what the grownups do. If you make a mistake using toys you can't get hurt. There's no boiling water in this pan, this iron isn't hot. But we like to pretend that it is, so we can copy grownups. We imitate what they do. *("Unplug" the iron.)*

When you grow up, do you think you'll know how to use a real iron? *(Nod your head to encourage the right response.)* Probably, because you've practiced with this toy iron. Will you be able to boil water without getting hurt, or saw and hammer wood? *(Pause for response.)* Maybe you'll be quite good at it, because you've had practice. You've copied grownups. You've imitated them, so you know the right way to do these things. We often learn by imitating, copying, others.

In fact, God wants us to imitate someone very special. He said, "Be imitators of God." That's how we can learn to live a good Christian life.

Jesus was God, wasn't he? *(Nod as you pause for response.)* Yes, he was! So, if we can imitate Jesus, if we can copy the way that Jesus lived, we'll be doing what God wants us to do.

What things can we do to imitate Jesus? *(Pause for response. You may want to get the children started with a few questions.)* Did Jesus love people? Yes, so we should try to love people, too. Was Jesus kind? We also should be kind to people. Was Jesus snooty, or was he a friend to all people? He was a friend to all; we should be, too.

How did Jesus say we should live? Should we be mean when people are mean to us? No! Jesus said to repay evil with goodness. If someone asks us to do something, Jesus said that we should do even more. Jesus said that we should treat people just exactly as we would like *(pause for response)* people to treat us.

If we do the things that Jesus said to do and live as he lived, we are imitating Jesus. Just as the Bible tells us to, we are imitating God.

These toys are nice. *(Indicate the toys.)* They're fun to play with and to learn with. Now, as you play with them, you know that you are copying, you are imitating, grownups. And that can remind you that you should always try to copy, to imitate, Jesus.

18

All Nature Sings

Scripture: *How many are your works, O LORD! In wisdom you made them all; the earth is full of your creatures* (Ps. 104:24).

Concept: By its very existence, *all* of creation praises God.

Objects: A jar containing some slightly moist soil, a few leaves, an earthworm, some ants, a spider. You can use some or all of these, or other common natural objects. Other objects, of course, will necessitate other facts.

Who would like to take a peek into this jar and tell me what they see? *(Show the children the jar and pause for response. Hand it to a child.)* Tell me one thing that you see in the jar.

(How you proceed, of course, is determined by the order in which the contents of the jar are listed. Stop whenever you feel you are running out of time or the children are losing interest. The idea is to tell at least one neat fact about each item, how that item fits into the world, and mention that God made that item.)

Dirt. There's more to that soil than just dirty dirt. Most dirt is filled with billions of tiny creatures, too small for us to see. They help keep the dirt healthy by eating dead things that fall onto the ground.

Healthy dirt is very important in this world. What are all of our trees and all of our plants planted in? *(Pause for response.)* Of course, dirt! If God didn't put dirt in the world, we probably couldn't have plants and trees. So you're looking at healthy dirt with lots of little critters in it, just the way God made it.

Leaves. Did you know that every single leaf you see is a tiny factory? That's right. God made every leaf so that it can take sunshine and make it into food for plants. Those leaves that you see are really tiny, living factories.

Why, do you think, did God give us leaves? *(Pause for response.)* For shade? Summer would be very hot without leaves on the trees, wouldn't it? Also, to make food for the plants. If God didn't make leaves, we wouldn't have many plants, and then *we* wouldn't have much food. So, when you look at leaves, you're looking at a very important part of creation.

Earthworm. A worm may be plain to us, but inside it's really very complicated. It has a stomach, intestines, a heart, and even nerves. We can't figure out exactly how it's created, it's so complicated. Only God knows that.

But we do know that God put worms here for a very special reason. They help make the soil good for growing plants. If God didn't give us worms, we'd

71

probably have a tough time growing food. So, when you look at a worm, you're looking at a very important piece of creation.

Ants. Did you know that there are over fourteen thousand different kinds of ants in the world? Some act like farmers and really grow little crops. Others take care of insects something like the way farmers take care of cows. Still others make slaves of other ants. Ants live in very complicated ant cities that we can hardly understand.

I'm glad that God made ants. They have a very important place in our world. If there were no ants in the woods, there would be a lot more bugs and fewer trees. If there were no ants in the ground, we'd need a lot more earthworms. Ants are part of the balance of creation.

Spiders. This is just a small spider, but I happen to know that it has at least two eyes, and maybe as many as eight. God gave each spider exactly the number of eyes that it needs. Spiders that don't weave webs have to see really well, so God gave most of them eight eyes. Some spiders are blind. They live in caves where it's too dark to see anything. So eyes wouldn't do them any good, would they?

Why, do you think, did God create spiders? *(Pause for response.)* Of course, to eat bugs. If God didn't give us spiders, we would have far too many insects in the world. Spiders are part of the balance of creation.

God made the whole world absolutely wonderful. Any creature that you look at, and even dirt and leaves and plants, have a place in creation. God made everything just right for its place.

Some people will tell you that the world just happened. But when you look closely you can see that God thought about it and made it just right.

The Bible says that the earth is full of God's creatures. It certainly is. And each creature, in its own way, praises God for the way he created it. We can look at all of creation—every little creature and even dirt—and praise God for how well he made it.

19

An Advertisement for God

Scripture: *In the same way, let your light shine before men, that they may see your good deeds and praise your Father in heaven* (Matt. 5:16).

Concept: The way we live should bring praise to God.

Objects: A picture of McDonald's golden arches and an empty Coke can. (This can be done with any recognizable product symbols.)

What does this remind you of? *(Show the McDonald's arches. Pause for response.)* How about hamburgers, McNuggets, and a shake? Sure! These are McDonald's golden arches. You recognize them right away, don't you? What do you think of when you see McDonald's? *(Pause for response.)* That's right, you think of fast food. You don't really think about the arches, do you? The golden arches now stand for food. See the arches and you think about food.

(Show the Coke can.) What do you think about when you see this? Sure, it's a Coke. You think about drinking a Coke. Although this can isn't the Coke itself, you immediately think of Coke because the can is such a good reminder. You recognize the color

of the can, you recognize the letters on the can, and you immediately forget about the can and think about Coke.

Even when this can is empty, it's advertising Coke. Just by being this can with the colors and letters it has on it, it's an ad for Coke.

Both of these *(hold up the arches picture and the can)* are good ads because everyone recognizes them. See the arches, think of McDonald's food. See the can, think of Coke to drink.

Did you ever think of yourself as a living advertisement? Of course, you're not a Coke can or a couple of golden arches. But, if you call yourself a Christian, you are advertising someone.

Whom are you advertising? *(Pause for response.)* Of course. When you say that you're a Christian, you're advertising Christ. He's in your name. And Christ, another name for Jesus, is God, so you're advertising for God.

You don't look like a bunch of ads to me. Tell me, how can you advertise for God? *(Pause for response. Discuss each response. If responses are not forthcoming, prompt the children with the following questions.)* Do you talk to people? Do you say naughty things, or is your talk nice? How would God want you to speak? No matter how you talk, if people know that you are a Christian, you're advertising God when you talk. People hear you talk and know that you're a Christian. So is keeping your talk clean a good ad for God? Of course!

How do you act toward people? Are you selfish and crabby, or are you generous and loving? What's a good ad for God? Sure! If you are generous and loving, you're doing what God wants you to.

(This can be a rather freewheeling discussion if you feel comfortable with that. The point is that all we do and say reflects on God if we call ourselves Christians. When it's time to stop, wrap it up with the final two paragraphs.)

God even told us in the Bible that we should not be afraid to let our lights shine but to do good deeds. Then people will see our good deeds, God said, and they will praise him, our Father in heaven.

This can *(hold up the Coke can)* advertises not a can but Coke. These arches *(hold up the picture)* don't advertise arches; they advertise McDonald's food. So you, a Christian, by your name advertise Christ. What you say and what you do advertise him. Are you going to be a good ad for Christ?

20

Bonsai Christians

Scripture: *Train a child in the way he should go, and when he is old he will not turn from it* (Prov. 22:6).

Concept: Your parents (or guardians) discipline you now so that you will become good Christians.

Object: A bonsai plant, available at most good nurseries. (This lesson can also be done with a picture of a trimmed hedge or shrub, or with the shrub itself. Note the changes at the end of this lesson.)

I brought this plant with me today especially to show you. *(Show the children the plant.)* The name isn't very important; but, does anyone know what this kind of plant is called? *(Pause only slightly for response so that the children don't lapse into a guessing game.)* It's called a bonsai. That's not really the name of the kind of plant. That refers to exactly what was done to this plant.

Do you think this little plant always looked so perfect? Did it grow exactly like this itself? *(Pause for response and shake your head to encourage the no.)* Of course not! This is a well-trimmed plant. It looks beautiful now, but it took a lot of work and probably many years to get it this way.

You see, this plant had the ability to grow all over the place. *(Indicate lots of branches and leaves with your hands.)* If left alone, it probably would have been big and bushy without much form to it.

But someone wanted it to look just like this. So every time a branch grew in the wrong place, that person snipped it off. *(Mimic the pruning of a branch.)* If too many leaves grew on this side, someone took off some of the leaves. *(Continue to mimic the pruning of the plant.)* If the plant bent toward the left, someone patiently eased it toward the right. The plant may have kept trying to grow all over the place, but someone was very patient in training it. And now you have this beautifully formed plant, this bonsai, that looks exactly the way someone wanted it to.

In a way you can think of yourself as this plant. Or better yet, you can think of yourself as this plant when it was young, before it looked exactly like this.

You probably have all sorts of things you want to try, and learn about and do, just as this plant had all sorts of directions in which it could grow.

But maybe some of the things you want to try aren't very good for young Christians to do. You're just a little young to know exactly what you should and should not do.

So you need someone to help you grow in the right direction, just as this plant needed someone to snip off branches and pull leaves and bend it to the right directions.

Who are the people who help you grow in the right direction? *(Pause for response. Using the plural* people *will help insure the answer parents. If you say per-* son, *you invite the answer God. If there are children not living with their parents in your audience, tailor the fol- lowing answer rather than the question.)* That's right, your parents! God put your parents, your mom or dad (grandma or grandpa, etc.) in charge of you to help you grow up. God even told your parents (grandparents or guardians) to train you to be good Christians.

That's why they discipline you at times. They may spank you or punish you for doing wrong, or not give you everything you want, or not let you do everything that you want to do. Sometimes it hurts a bit, just as trimming a branch from this plant *(indi- cate the plant)* isn't all that pleasant. But in the end you'll be a better Christian because of their training.

So when your parents (or guardians, etc.) won't let you do just anything, or when they punish you for doing something wrong, think of this plant and how good it looks. Then you can remember that they want you to become a good Christian.

And next time you see a bonsai plant like this, you can appreciate all the work that went into training it. And you can thank God for parents (guardians, etc.) who love you and want to train you in the right way.

Option

If you use a picture of a shrub, mention the fact once that it's a picture. Then talk about it as if it's the full shrub in front of you, substituting the word *shrub* for plant, bonsai, and bonsai plant.

If you draw a picture of a shrub, try to copy one that's included in your church's landscaping. Mention that fact at the beginning. Then at the end you can say, "And, next time you come to church and see that hedge at the corner . . ."

If you use this with children alone rather than in front of a congregation, you can take the children outside and seat them near a particular shrub.

If you use a potted shrub, be sure that it's well trimmed.

21

Fitted Together

Scripture: *From him the whole body, joined and held together by every supporting ligament, grows and builds itself up in love, as each part does its work* (Eph. 4:16).

Concept: Each of us has a place in the church.

Object: An unfinished jigsaw puzzle, with a few loose pieces in a bag. (This works best if you have a simple puzzle that fits into its own board. If you have a piece for each child, you could put a name on the back of each piece. See option.)

I started a puzzle this week but didn't get it finished, so I brought it along. *(Show the unfinished puzzle.)* Maybe we can put in a few pieces together.

But then, maybe we shouldn't. Maybe this is finished just the way it is. Do you think this puzzle looks finished? *(Show the puzzle again, shake your head as you speak, and pause for response.)* No! It's missing a few pieces. A puzzle isn't complete until all the pieces are in place, is it?

(Take a piece from the bag and hold it for the children to see.) Can you tell what this is? *(Pause for response.)* Well, yes, it's a piece of the puzzle. Can you tell what part of the picture it is? *(Pause for response.)* No, not really. This is not good by itself, is it? It doesn't make the complete picture by itself. It's a piece of the puzzle. It works best in the puzzle.

Let's see where it goes. *(Try a few places.)* Not here; it's the wrong shape. Not here; the picture doesn't look right. Here it goes! *(Put the piece into place, show the puzzle, and point out the piece.)* It fits perfectly in here. No other piece would fit here. This is its place, all right. Every piece has its own place, doesn't it?

(Pick one of the larger pieces and hold it up.) This looks like an important piece, it's so large. Is this an especially important piece? *(Pause for response.)* Well, maybe and maybe not. We'll see.

(Pick another piece from the bag and hold it up next to the last piece.) This is a little smaller. Maybe it's not as important. Do you think this *(hold up the bigger piece)* piece is more important than this *(hold up the smaller piece)* piece? *(Pause for response.)* No! The puzzle needs both of them, doesn't it? No piece is more important than another piece. Every piece is equally important to complete the puzzle. *(If the puzzle is incomplete, finish it while you are talking.)*

(Show the completed puzzle.) I brought this puzzle along today because I wanted to talk about our church. That sounds strange, doesn't it? I want to pretend for a minute that this *(indicate the complete*

puzzle) is our church, right here: (<u>Name of your church</u>) Church. *(Indicate the sanctuary and the people.)* We're a complete Christian church, just as this is a complete puzzle. And these *(pick out a few pieces and hold them up)* are all the people—you, me, and everybody out there.

Option

(Turn some pieces over to show some names.) In fact, your names are on these pieces. Here's Jason, Cara, Mitchell, Lucas. Everybody here is a piece of this puzzle, because everybody here is a part of this church.

(If you have a visitor, you can ask his or her name and mention that that name is probably on a piece of another puzzle. If the child is an unchurched visitor, maybe the name is on one of these pieces and we just don't know it. Or, the name is on the big puzzle of all of God's children.)

Continue Lesson

(Put pieces back into the puzzle as you speak the following paragraphs, but don't complete it.) The Bible says that we all have a place in Jesus' church. *(Show the incomplete puzzle.)* The church isn't complete without each one of us. Each of us is important to Jesus. *(Pick up a couple of pieces.)*

And we're all different, aren't we? *(Hold up the two pieces and point out the different shapes.)* Maybe you can sing well, Susie *(no names of children present)* can draw well, Ralph is smart, and Tina is

83

friendly. God made each of us to be different from every other person.

(Fit those pieces into place.) Yet there's a certain place for each one of us. You can sing in the choir, Susie can help make banners, Ralph can help us understand things, and Tina can welcome new people.

(Hold up a big piece.) Some of us may *seem* more important than others. Maybe you hear about (name of your pastor and/or other people prominent in your congregation), but they don't make the complete picture, do they? *(Hold up the incomplete puzzle.)*

We all have a place. God gave each of us gifts that we can use for him. Jesus' whole church isn't complete without us. *(Complete the puzzle as you speak. If you have names on the pieces, pause here to call out the names as you put the pieces in place.)*

(Show the completed puzzle.) See how all the shapes fit perfectly together? Each has its own place. That's like the church. Everybody together, using their talents for Jesus. You *(point at some and sweep your arm to indicate all of them)* are important to Jesus in his church.

The next time you work a puzzle or see someone working one, you can think of Jesus and his church. All the pieces fit together perfectly. All the pieces are important. Every one of you *(indicate all the children)* is an important piece in that puzzle.

22

Taking Revenge

Scripture: *Do not take revenge, my friends, but leave room for God's wrath, for it is written: "It is mine to avenge; I will repay," says the Lord. . . . Do not be overcome by evil, but overcome evil with good* (Rom. 12:19, 21).

Concept: We should not take revenge on those who wrong us; rather, we should treat them kindly.

Object: A wasp, a bee, or some other stinging insect in a jar. (With a few adjustments, you can do this lesson with a picture of a stinging insect.)

I had to be very careful when I caught this wasp yesterday. (*Show the wasp.*) It became angry and tried to sting me. I don't blame it. I would be angry, too, if someone caught me and put me in a big jar. Wouldn't you?

Usually we don't have to worry about wasps, or bees, or things that sting. If we ignore them or treat them with respect, they generally don't sting. But

85

when they become angry, or feel that they're in danger, watch out! That's when they sting.

I probably can make this wasp angry by shaking the jar a bit. *(Shake the jar, and show the wasp again.)* Of course, I wouldn't like to be in a jar that someone was shaking. We'll let it calm down a bit. *(Put the jar down.)*

How many of you have been stung by a wasp or bee? *(Raise your hand as you ask, encouraging the children to do likewise. Do not pause for response. Simply acknowledge the raised hands.)* I'll bet that you may have stepped on it or bothered it in some way so that it became angry and stung. That's a natural reaction for wasps and bees. They think they're in danger or they get angry, so they fight back.

That's a natural reaction for us, too, isn't it? Of course, we can't sting. But when someone does something mean to us, we want to fight back, right? We're angry and we want to get back at them.

If you're playing with a toy, and someone takes that toy away, what do you want to do? Most people would yell and grab the toy back, right?

Or, if you're minding your own business at school and someone calls you a nasty name, what do you want to do? Call them the same name or a worse name? Most people would.

We're just like this wasp *(show the wasp, shake the jar)*, stinging when it's angry. We want to get back at people who are mean to us. Getting back at people feels almost as natural as this wasp stinging when it's angry. Someone's mean to you and—Blammo!—you sock it to them; you get back.

Do you know what the Bible says about getting back at people? It tells us not to do it. Don't try to get back at people, even when they're mean to you. The Bible tells us to leave all the getting back at people to God. If they're mean to you, let it go. Or, better yet, be good to them. That's very hard to do, isn't it?

So, when someone takes away a toy that you are playing with *(shake the jar)*, instead of getting back, what can you do? *(Pause for response. You may have to lead with questions.)* Would God want you to grab the toy back? No. Rather, explain that you both can play with the toy, that you want to share or take turns with your toys. Better yet, you might tell her she can have the toy and share it with you. That's really being good to her, isn't it?

Or, when someone calls you a name *(shake the jar again)*, will you yell back at him? *(Pause for response.)* No! Pay no attention. That's hard to do, but give it a try. Better yet, try being kind to him. Paying back meanness with kindness just may make him your friend. God tells us to pay back evil with good.

I'm going to leave this jar alone for a while now. *(Put the jar away.)* The wasp will calm down. Then it won't be so liable to sting when I let it out today. If you happen to see it flying outside, don't make it angry. If you do, it will sting; that's natural for it.

Instead, let it remind you that God doesn't want us to be waspish Christians. God tells us not to get back at people. Rather, be a gentle Christian and repay, even when someone is mean, with kindness.

23

Washed by Christ

Scripture: *The blood of Jesus, his Son, purifies us from all sin* (1 John 1:7).

Concept: Jesus' blood can wash away our sins.

Objects: A water-soluble marker, a jar of water, a small towel

I'm going to give you a little demonstration today and help you guess what I'm talking about. I'll give you a few hints along the way, so listen closely.

(Show the palm of your hand.) We're going to pretend that this is my soul. You can't see my soul; no one but God can see souls. A soul is inside of you, the living part of you. So this *(show your palm again)* is going to stand for my soul.

It's nice and clean right now, without any spots, isn't it? But my soul—anybody's soul—isn't always nice and clean. Sometimes we do bad things or think bad thoughts. That's not right. That's like a stain or a spot on a soul.

So now I'm going to pretend that this *(show your clean palm)*, my clean soul, is stained or spotted with sin. *(Take the marker and write "sin" on your palm while you talk.)* I did something wrong. I sinned. So now there is sin in my soul. *(Show your palm with "sin" written on it.)*

But, I'm sorry for what I did. I'd like to take back those words that I said. I'd like to undo the bad thing that I did. So I'll try to take it back and undo it all by myself. I'll try to take that sin out of my soul. *(Take the dry cloth and rub your palm with it while you speak.)* Do you think I can rub this spot off with a dry cloth? Can I take that sin out of my soul all by myself? *(Pause for response.)* No, I can't take back what I did. I can't rub this spot out. *(Show your palm.)*

What should I use to get this mark off my hand? What should I use to wash my hand? *(Pause for response as you reveal the jar of water.)* Water, of course! Water helps wash away all sorts of dirty things.

(Dip part of the towel in water to wet it. Make sure you have enough water on it.) I can't do it alone. I need the water. *(Rub the mark off your hand with the wet towel. Don't be alarmed if it doesn't all come off at first. Hold your hand up for the children to see.)* The water is doing its job already. The mark has started to come off.

(Continue to work on the mark as you speak.) But this isn't really my soul, is it? And that marker isn't really sin, is it? I just put marker on my hand so that you could see it. I did that so you could understand how sin marks our souls.

Now, here's where I want you to guess. If my hand stood for my soul, and this marker stood for sin, what, do you think, does the water stand for? What or who is the only thing that can take away our sins? *(Pause for response. Some children may say Jesus. If not, say, "Who takes away our sin?" Pick up the thought where appropriate.)* That's right, God does! Was Jesus God? Of course! Then, does Jesus take away our sins? Yes! What did Jesus do to take away our sins? He died for us! Sometimes we say that Jesus shed his blood for our sins. So, does Jesus' blood wash away our sins? Yes! That's the only thing that can clean sin from our souls—Jesus' blood.

We can't get rid of our sins by ourselves. *(Rub your palm with a finger or the dry part of the towel.)* Only Jesus' blood can wash them away. *(Wet towel on your hand.)* And if we believe that Jesus died for our sins, that blood he shed so long ago still washes the sin from our souls.

If we believe in Jesus, God looks at our souls and sees clean souls. *(Show your cleaned palm. If it isn't completely clean, say, "God doesn't even see this much sin. He sees a clean soul," and show your other palm.)* Our souls are washed in Jesus' blood.

So, the next time you have to wash your hands or rub some stain off them, remember to use water. And then you can remember that Jesus' blood washes us on the inside, better than water does on the outside.

24

Color Your World for Jesus

Scripture: *Don't you know that a little yeast works through the whole batch of dough?* (1 Cor. 5:6).

Concept: The little things you do make a difference.

Objects: A jar of water and a bottle of red food coloring. (This can be done with any color food coloring. You will have to change a few sentences.)

I was making a little food for my hummingbird feeder this week, so I brought it along to show you something neat. *(Show the jar of water.)* This is the food. It's going to be sugar water that hummingbirds like.

These birds like red things. They come naturally to red. So most people color their water red to attract the birds. How can I make this water red? *(Pause for response.)*

(Show the food coloring.) Here's the easiest way to do it. This is food coloring, but it also colors water. If I pour this *(indicate the coloring)* into here *(indicate the jar of water)*, I'll have the red water.

Now here's the neat thing I wanted to show you. Just a little tiny bit of this *(indicate the coloring)* will turn all of this *(indicate the jar of water)* red. Watch this. I'll pour in one drop *(carefully pour one drop of coloring into the water; hold the water jar high, so all the children can easily see the coloring work)*. See what it does?

The one drop doesn't sit there all by itself. It spreads. It affects the whole jar of water. Look at what one more drop will do. *(Put one more drop of coloring into the water and hold it high.)*

The Bible talks about this very thing. It doesn't say, "A little red food coloring can color a whole jar of water." But it says something very close. It says, "A little yeast works through the whole batch of dough." People use yeast when they bake bread. It's as neat as this food coloring. A little bit spreads through the whole loaf of bread. That's just like one drop of food coloring *(put another drop of color into the water)* changing the color of all this water.

But the Bible doesn't really talk about yeast or food coloring. It talks about the neat things they do and compares that to what we do. The Bible says little things that we do can color the world around us.

Let me explain that. Let's say that you want to color your world for Jesus. You want to make a difference. Now, you're only a child; do you think you can make a big difference? The Bible says yes. Here's how.

(Hold up your jar and the food coloring. Every time you mention an action by a child, put one drop of coloring into the water.)

You come to church happy and smiling *(drop of color)*. Someone sees you smile, and that makes them feel happy. So they smile. Pretty soon everyone around you is smiling. You've colored your world with a smile.

You tell your friends that Jesus loves us *(drop of color)*. They tell their friends, and they tell their friends, and so on. You've colored your world for Jesus. *(Put the equipment down here until you have a list of things to do for Jesus.)*

What kinds of things does Jesus want you to do? *(Pause for response. Prompt the children with these questions.)* Does Jesus want you to be kind? Does he want you to be generous? Does he want you to love your neighbors? The little things you do make a big difference. *(Pick up the equipment.)* You can color your world for Jesus.

When you are kind *(put in a drop of color)*, other people see that and often act kindly, too. When you are generous *(put in another drop of color)*, people learn to share. When you love someone *(put in another drop of color)* and show it, you're spreading love in your world. You are coloring your world for Jesus.

Look at what all those drops of color did! *(Hold the jar high.)* They certainly colored the water. Just like that, you can color your world for Jesus.

The next time you see some colored punch or juice or chocolate milk or even a hummingbird feeder *(hold the jar high)*, you can think of the little bit of coloring that went into it and how it colored everything. Then remember that you can color your world for Jesus.

25

Rules of the Game

Scripture: *In everything, do to others what you would have them do to you, for this sums up the Law and the Prophets* (Matt. 7:12).

Concept: Jesus' main rule for our lives is to treat others the way we want to be treated.

Objects: A few simple games, such as Old Maid and Go Fish, with their lists of rules, and a Bible. (Before you give this lesson, find some of the more complicated rules in one of the easy games. Condense those rules and write them down.)

I bought a few games at the store this week and thought that you might like to see them.

(Show the Old Maid game.) This is Old Maid. How many of you know how to play Old Maid? *(Raise your hand as you ask the question to encourage a similar response.)* Well, for those of you who don't, there's a list of rules. Let me read you some of them. *(Read a few of the rules.)* Sounds like fun, doesn't it? If you read the rules, or someone tells you the rules, you can learn to play this game.

Here's another one. *(Show the Go Fish cards.)* This is Go Fish. How many of you know how to play this? *(Raise your hand as you ask the question to encourage a similar response.)* Well, for those of you who don't, there's a list of rules. Let me read you some of them. *(Read a few of the rules.)* Sounds like fun, doesn't it? If you read the rules, or someone tells you the rules, you can learn to play this game.

(Continue in this manner until you've gone through your games, but keep it brief.)

It looks as if for each game there's a set of rules. If you don't know how to play, read the rules or have someone tell you. Then you can play the game.

Sometimes the rules sound a little complicated, don't they? Here are a few from Old Maid (or one of the games most kids play without rules). *(Read some of the more complicated rules.)* I think that sounds harder than the game is. We can make that easier. That simply means, *(read your condensed list of rules).* That's easier, isn't it? It means the same thing.

How many of you have played Old Maid without reading the rules? *(Raise your hand as you speak to encourage a like response. Continue speaking.)* You probably started with someone who knew how to play, and they told you how, right? That's the way it is with a lot of games. Someone just tells you the rules and you learn as you go.

Yet, there are rules, aren't there? *(Hold up the lists of rules.)* There's always a certain way to play a game. Those are the rules.

We have rules in our lives, too, don't we? There's a certain way we should live. Those are the rules.

Where can we find the rules for our lives? *(Hold up the Bible as you ask the question, and pause for response.)* That's right, in the Bible! God tells us in the Bible how to live. That's where God gives us the rules.

You shall not kill. You shall not steal. Love one another. Those are a few of our rules. Can you think of any others? *(Pause for response and repeat each child's response.)* What did Jesus teach us? We should be kind. We should be generous. We should love one another.

That's a lot of rules, isn't it? Just as these *(indicate a list of rules)* tell you the best way to play a game, the Bible *(hold up the Bible)* has a lot of rules and suggestions for the best way to live.

But, if that seems really complicated, Jesus made it all very simple. Instead of telling you a lot of rules like someone telling you how to play a game, Jesus summed up all God's rules in one sentence. In fact, sometimes we call it the Golden Rule.

Jesus said that we should treat others how? *(Pause for response.)* That's right. We should treat others just like we want others to treat us.

Do you want people to be nice to you? *(Nod your head and pause for response.)* Of course! Then, Jesus said, you should be nice to people.

Do you want people to play with you and share their toys? *(Nod and pause for response.)* Yes! Then play with others and share your things.

Do you want people to love you? *(Nod and pause for response.)* Of course. Then, Jesus said, you should show love to them.

It's all very simple. It's like the short form of all the rules for living. *(Hold up the Bible and a list of rules.)* Jesus told you to do to others exactly what you want them to do to you.

That's easy to remember, isn't it? You can even remember that when you play these games *(indicate the games)* with your friends. Do to them what you want them to do to you. Then you're living the way Jesus wants you to live.

26

Looking on the Inside

Scripture: *The LORD does not look at the things man looks at. Man looks at the outward appearance, but the LORD looks at the heart* (1 Sam. 16:7).

Concept: God looks at our hearts, not our outward appearances.

Objects: A banana, an orange, a grapefruit, some peanuts, a coconut (any good food that has a hard or thick rind or shell)

I want to find out some of your likes and dislikes this morning. Also, I want to know a little bit about why you like some things. You don't have to like all of these. You may like some and not like others at all; that's perfectly fine. To show that you like something, raise your hand.

(Hold up the banana.) Who likes bananas? *(Raise your hand as you ask to encourage that response.)* Good! Maybe not everybody, but a lot of you like bananas. There's a little spot on this one, but I'm sure it's OK inside, and that's what counts.

(Hold up the orange.) Who likes oranges? *(Continue in this manner until you have gone through all the foods.*

Comment on each one just a bit. If there's a blemish on the outside, be sure to mention it in passing, but say that it's probably fine on the inside.)

Look at this banana. *(Hold it up alone.)* Does this whole thing look good to eat, spot and all? *(Pause for response.)* No! I wouldn't want to eat a banana peel. And the spot doesn't make it look very good. Do you eat the outside or the inside of the banana? *(Pause for response.)* The inside, of course! The outside doesn't make any difference. You look at a banana, and you know what's on the inside. That's what you like.

(Hold up as much of the other fruit as possible.) How do you know that you like grapefruit, or oranges, or peanuts? Some of you think these are very good. You don't know just by looking at them, do you? *(Shake your head but don't pause.)* Not really. The outside doesn't make any difference. You know you like one because you have eaten the inside of one like it. Look at any of these foods and you think about the inside, not the outside. Does the outside make any difference to you? *(Pause for response.)* Of course not! Would it matter if this orange were purple, as long as there was an orange inside that peel? *(Pause for response.)* No! It would still be an orange.

What's important: how the outside looks, or what's on the inside? *(Pause for response.)* Of course. It's what's on the inside that counts.

That's exactly what God says. But he doesn't say that about food; he says that about people. God says that it's what's in your heart that counts. He says that people look at the outward appearance—what you look like—but God looks at your heart.

You may look in a mirror and think that you are ugly. I look at you and I don't think any of you are ugly; you're all good-looking in your own ways. But God doesn't even see that. God looks straight at your heart.

So, does what you look like really matter? *(Shake your head as you pause for response.)* Does what you wear matter at all to God? *(Pause for response.)* Does God love you more if you are absolutely beautiful and have lots and lots of friends? *(Pause for response.)* Of course not. God looks only at your heart. He loves you for yourself, not at all for what you look like. He looks at the real you, your heart, to see if you love him. That's what matters.

Just as you can "look" right through the peels of bananas, or oranges, or grapefruit *(hold up the banana)* and know that you like them, God looks inside of you. He doesn't care at all what the outer you looks like. And he knows that he loves you.

27

Put On that Headset!

Scripture: *He who belongs to God hears what God says* (John 8:47).

We must pay more careful attention, therefore, to what we have heard, so that we do not drift away (Heb. 2:1).

Concept: We should pay close attention to what God says.

Object: A Walkman-type radio with a headset. (Check ahead of time to be sure you get radio reception inside the building.)

Here's my favorite little personal radio. *(Show the radio without the headset.)* It doesn't give a big sound, but I can hear it quite well. *(Turn the radio on rather softly and listen for a minute.)* Can you hear it? *(If someone in the back can't hear, turn up the volume a bit.)* If we sit still and listen, we can hear it all right, can't we?

But very few of us sit still and listen to a radio all day. We like to play and talk to other people. There are things we want to do and things we have to do every day. Sometimes, even if the radio is on, like it is now, we can't always hear it. Can you listen to the radio right now, when I'm talking? *(Shake your head and pause for response.)* No. Sometimes we have to be quiet and *try* to hear the radio.

(Show the headset.) Now, this is a handy gadget. Can anyone tell me what it is? *(Pause for response.)* Yes, it's a headset. How do we use this? *(Pause for response.)* That's right, we plug it into the radio and put it over our ears. *(Demonstrate as you speak.)* Now I can hear the radio very well. Even if you talk, or if we do things, I'll still be able to hear the radio. *(Take off the headset.)*

Lots of people use headsets like this. Joggers often use headsets when they're running. How many of you have seen people with headsets on? *(Raise your hand to encourage that response.)* Sure. The next time you see someone running down the street, or even walking, check to see if they have a headset. That means that they really want to listen to the radio. They want to pay close attention to it, so they put on the headset.

How many of you have a headset like this? *(Raise your hand and pause for response.)* That's what I thought. Not everybody owns a headset. But we can pretend that we do.

Let's pretend for a minute. Pretend that you have a headset and you want to hear something very important. Put on your headset like this. *(Pretend to put on a headset and encourage the children to pretend.)* Are you ready? Here comes an important announcement. *(Speak like an announcer.)* Jesus said that whoever belongs to God listens to what God says. Stay tuned for further announcements.

Did you hear that? Of course, you heard because you were listening closely. Put your headset on again. *(Pretend to put on a headset.)* Here comes an important announcement. Are you ready? *(Speak like an announcer.)* We must pay careful attention to what God says.

Did you hear that? Sure, you had your headset on.

The Bible says that we should hear what God says and pay careful attention. That's like putting on a pretend headset so that other things don't bother us.

How can we pay close attention to what God says? *(Pause for response. Prompt the children with questions. Every time you mention a way to pay attention, pretend you are putting on a headset.)* Should we listen to the Bible stories we hear? Should we pray to God and ask him to help us pay attention? Should we listen in church and Sunday school? Should we listen when our parents tell us about God?

Those are all ways that we can pay close attention to what God says. Every time we listen closely, we put on a pretend headset. We ignore other things and voices and listen closely to what God says.

So, we don't really need a headset, do we? We can pretend that we have one by paying close attention to what God says. And when we see someone else using a real headset *(show the headset)*, that can remind us always to pay close attention to what God says to us.

28

Looking to Jesus

Scripture: *Let us fix our eyes on Jesus, the author and perfecter of our faith* (Heb. 12:2).

Concept: To live well, keep your mind fixed on Jesus.

Object: A houseplant which is obviously bending in one direction. (Set it with only one side facing the sun for a while. A sun-loving leggy plant works best.)

See how crooked this plant is growing? *(Show the plant.)* What, do you suppose, happened to it? *(Pause for response.)*

Shall I tell you? Only one side faced the sun. I didn't turn it around often enough.

The plant was here *(hold up the plant),* and the window was here *(indicate on which side of the plant the sun shone).* So it bent toward where the sun was coming from.

If I had turned it around once in a while, it would have grown straight. First it would have bent this way toward the sun, but when I turned it around, it would have had to bend this way. *(Hold the plant up. Indicate where the sun came from. Then turn the plant so the children can see how it would bend.)* So it would have grown quite straight.

There's something in most plants that turns toward the sun, that seeks the sun. Sunlight is very important to most plants. They die without it. And they try their hardest to turn themselves toward the sun, just like this one did. They know what's good for them, and they almost look for it.

In fact, this plant can remind us that we should do the same thing. We should know what's good for us and look for it and try to face it.

Who is the best person who ever lived in this world? Who is it best for us to follow? *(Pause for response.)* Jesus, of course.

In fact, Jesus is like the sun for our Christian lives. He gives us everything that we need to live as good Christians.

And, just as this plant can't live without sun, we can't live without Jesus, can we? Who saved us from our sins? *(Pause for response.)* Jesus! Who gives us eternal life in heaven? *(Pause for response.)* Jesus! Without him we can't live as Christians, can we? He's our sun.

The Bible tells us to fix our eyes on Jesus. We really can't see him with our eyes right now, can we? *(Shake your head and pause for response.)* No.

But we can look at Jesus with our hearts. We can think about him and love him. We can pray to him and try to please him. That's what the Bible means when it tells us to fix our eyes on him. We'll look at Jesus with our hearts.

That's just like this plant *(hold up the plant)* looking for the sun. It tries its hardest to "look" toward the sun for life. And we can try our hardest to look to Jesus with our hearts.

How many of you have plants around the house? *(Raise your hand as you ask the question and pause for response.)* Good. Maybe you can try a little experiment on them. Maybe an adult can help you.

This week take one out of the sunshine. Put it in a shadow, but near the sun. Watch it every day and see if it bends, or "looks," toward the sun. Then, every day when you look at it, you can remind yourself to bend toward Jesus, to look toward him and to love him in your heart.

29

God's How-to Book

Scripture: *All Scripture is God-breathed and is useful for teaching, rebuking, correcting and training in righteousness, so that the man of God may be thoroughly equipped for every good work* (2 Tim. 3:16–17).

Concept: The Bible tells us how to live a life pleasing to God.

Objects: An unassembled toy with instructions on how to put it together, a cookbook, a how-to book, a Bible. (You can use almost any kind of directions or how-to books. What you say depends, of course, on the books you use. The example below uses an unassembled pogo stick, a cookbook, and a how-to book. The idea is to impress the children with the fact that you don't know how to do something and you have only one chance to get it right.)

See what I bought at the store this week! *(Show the toy in the package.)* It's a pogo stick (or whatever). *(If there's a picture of it assembled, let the children see the picture.)* When I bought it, I thought I was getting this whole pogo stick, ready to use.

When I got it home, I saw that I had to put it together myself. *(Look perplexed.)*

I paid quite a bit for this pogo stick; I can't afford to buy another one. So I can't ruin this with a mistake. I've got to do it right when I put it together.

How can I put this together? I don't know the first thing about making pogo sticks. What can I do? *(Pause for response, then show the instructions.)* I'm really fortunate that someone included instructions with this thing. It tells me, step by step, how to put it together. It was probably written by a pogo stick expert. If I follow what that person wrote, I should get it right.

I've got another little problem. This is more difficult than putting a pogo stick together. An old friend of mine is coming over. She loves butter brickle cake, so I'm going to bake one for her. I've never done it before, and I've got to get that right on the first try, because my friend will have the first piece. How can I make that cake when I've never made it before now? *(Show the cookbook and pause for response.)* You're right! I'll follow the directions in this cookbook. *(Show the recipe and read part of it.)* There are even pictures in the front of the book that show me exactly how to do certain things. Some expert cook wrote this for people like me to follow. I've only got one chance with that cake, but I think I'll get it right if I follow that recipe.

This problem is tougher yet. My friend and I are going to build a tree house. Neither of us has done it before, but we've got to do it right. Neither of us wants it to fall out of the tree. We've got one week, one chance, to build that tree house right. How can we do that?

(Pause for response and get out the how-to book.) Now you've got the idea! I went to the library and got this how-to book. It tells me exactly how to make a tree house. There are even pictures in it, in case I don't understand the instructions. *(Show the pictures.)* If we follow these instructions exactly, we should have a fine tree house.

Maybe I could have gotten another pogo stick, or baked another cake, or even hired someone to make that tree house. But now we've got a really tough problem: Everyone only has one chance to do this one thing right, and each of us has to do it alone.

Can anyone live your life for you? *(Shake your head as you ask, to elicit the proper response.)* No! Only you can live your life. Do you get a second chance? Do you have two lives? *(Shake your head again.)* No! We all have one life, so we want to live it right.

Is there a set of directions for living our lives? Do we have a book of instructions from an expert who knows all about life? *(Nod as you ask the questions.)* Yes, we do! We've got a perfect set of instructions in the Bible. *(Show the Bible.)*

Who gave us the Bible? *(Pause for response.)* God did! So, if we want to live a life that pleases God, the Bible is the perfect set of instructions.

Can you think of some instructions the Bible gives us? Love one another. Do extra things for people. Honor your parents. *(If you prompt the children, try to use positive instructions rather than the "Thou shalt nots.")* That's right; the Bible gives us many instructions on how to live. We each have one life; God wants us to live it right, so he gave us the perfect how-to-do-it book.

It's a good idea to use instructions or how-to books when you do new things. *(Show the instructions, cookbook, etc.)* You'll probably use things like this once in a while. And these can remind you that this *(show the Bible)* is God's instruction book for your life. This is a book you should use all the time.

30

Weeding Our Gardens

Scripture: *Therefore each of you must put off falsehood and speak truthfully to his neighbor. . . . Do not let the sun go down while you are still angry. . . . He who has been stealing must steal no longer. . . . Do not let any unwholesome talk come out of your mouths. . . . Get rid of all bitterness, rage and anger. . . . Be kind and compassionate to one another, forgiving each other, just as in Christ God forgave you* (Eph. 4:25–32).

Concept: We should all try to get rid of bad character traits.

Object: A potted houseplant with a few weeds shooting up. (References to weeding outdoor gardens work well only in season.)

I was taking care of my plants yesterday and found this one that needs some work. *(Show the plant and point out the weeds as you speak.)* The plant looks fine right now, but I think I should weed it.

See these extra little shoots? They're weeds in this pot. They're not part of the plant. If I let them grow, the plant won't be as healthy as it should be. These little weeds will take some of the water I give the plant. They'll take some healthy minerals from the soil. They'll take space in the pot where the plant should grow. They may even grow big enough to take over the pot; then my plant would die.

Option 1

(Add the next four sentences now if you are not making reference to outdoor gardens.) What should I do about these weeds? *(Pause for response.)* That's right, I should pull them out. We call that weeding. I should weed this plant.

Option 2

The same thing is happening in our outdoor gardens right now. The flowers and vegetables we planted last spring are growing nicely. But weeds are growing in the gardens, too. If the weeds grow, our vegetables and flowers won't be as healthy as they should be. What should we do about weeds in our gardens? What should I do about the weeds in this pot? *(Pause for response.)* That's right, we should pull out the weeds. We call that weeding our gardens. People have been weeding their gardens lately. I should weed this plant, too.

Continue Lesson

There's something else that we all should weed. That's ourselves! It sounds funny to weed yourself, doesn't it? We're not plants that grow in gardens or pots, but we do have to weed ourselves. Let me explain.

Pretend that you're this plant. *(Hold the pot high and indicate the plant as you speak.)* You're growing up straight and tall, a good person living the way God wants you to live.

But then you start telling lies. *(Indicate one of the weeds.)* "I didn't do that." "I didn't say that." That isn't good, is it? *(Shake your head and pause for response.)* No, that's like a weed. If you keep lying, you're not going to be a very good person, are you?

So, what should you do about lying? *(Pause for response.)* You should stop lying, right? You should tell the truth all the time. When you stop lying *(pull out the weed)*, you're weeding yourself so that you can grow up right.

Or, say, you start acting selfish. *(Indicate another weed.)* That's not good, is it? *(Shake your head and pause for response.)* No, that's another weed. What should you do? *(Pause for response.)* That's right! *(Pull the weed out as you speak.)* Stop being selfish and learn to share your things. Pull out that weed so that you can grow well.

One more. Suppose you say bad, nasty things. *(Indicate a weed.)* Another weed in your life? *(Nod your head and pause for response.)* That surely is. God wants only good language to come from your mouth. What should you do? *(Pause for response.)* Yes! Stop your bad language and say only good and true things. *(Pull the weed.)* Weed out your language so that you can grow into a good Christian.

When all the weeds are out, there's room to grow as kind, loving, generous Christians. That's the way God wants us to grow.

Option 2

Watch people in their gardens this week. They'll probably be out there weeding. That's the thing to do right now.

And that's the thing that we should always do in our lives. We should try to keep our own gardens and plants—us—weeded and growing right for God.

Continue Lesson

I'm going to finish weeding this plant when I get home. I want to remind myself that we all have to weed our lives, get rid of our bad habits, to grow right for God.

31

Think Like a Sieve

Scripture: *Finally, brothers, whatever is true, whatever is noble, whatever is right, whatever is pure, whatever is lovely, whatever is admirable—if anything is excellent or praiseworthy—think about such things* (Phil. 4:8).

Concept: Let bad thoughts go; concentrate on good thoughts.

Objects: A sieve (a colander will do); two paper bags, one holding a handful of sand and pebbles. (Instead of sand and pebbles, you can use sugar with hard lumps or flour with something hidden in it. The idea is to have two things that can be separated with a sieve. Be careful that the larger object isn't necessarily "bad," as in sifting impurities from flour.)

Does anyone know what this is? *(Hold up the sieve for all the children to see. Pause for and repeat the responses.)* It's a sieve (pronounced siv). What is it used for? *(Pause for response and repeat the responses.)* That's right. It's used to separate small things from bigger things. It's often used in the kitchen. Let me show you how it works.

(Hold up the bag containing the sand.) I've got some sand from a sandbox in here. But there also are some small stones. I want those stones; I can put the sand back in the sandbox. So I'll put it all through the sieve. *(Position the sieve beneath the bag of sand, with the empty bag beneath the sieve. Try to keep the sieve high enough for all the children to see as you pour the sand through the sieve.)* The sand pours through, but the stones are caught by the sieve. *(Show the stones in the sieve.)* Here are my stones, and here *(indicate the bag of sand)* is the sand. Now I can use the stones. This sieve is a handy little gadget for separating things. *(After you show them, put the stones back into the sand as you speak.)*

Sometimes I think it would be nice to have a sieve like this in our heads. Do you know what I'd like to separate in my head? I would like to separate my thoughts.

(Demonstrate with the sieve and the empty bag as you speak.) I'd like to take all my thoughts and dump them into this sieve, then let the sieve separate my bad and gloomy thoughts from my good and cheerful thoughts. I could throw the bad and gloomy thoughts away and think only good and cheerful thoughts. That would be neat, wouldn't it?

God wants us to think good and cheerful thoughts. He said in the Bible that we should think about things that are true, right, excellent, and worthy of praise. He wants us to put bad thoughts right out of our minds.

What are some good thoughts? Can you tell me? *(Pause for response. Repeat each response so that everyone can hear it. If no response is forthcoming, prompt the children with the following thoughts.)* Here are some: Johnny is a nice person. Look at those beautiful flowers. God made a good world. Jesus loves me. I want to please Jesus. God gave me a wonderful family. How can I help my neighbor? God is love.

That's right! Those are all good thoughts. We're not even going to talk about the bad and gloomy thoughts, because God doesn't want us to think them. So we're going to sift them right out without even looking at them.

(Run the sand through the sieve once more. Keep the sieve close enough to the empty bag so that the children don't see the sand. Then hold up the sieve with the pebbles.) Here we are, all the good thoughts. Here's "God is love." Here's "Johnny is a nice person." *(With each thought mentioned, pick a pebble from the sieve, show it to the children, and put it aside. Continue this as long as you like.)*

Handy thing, this sieve. *(Hold up the sieve.)* It would be nice for each of us to have one in our heads to separate our thoughts. But we don't, do we? So we'll just have to use this as a reminder to think only good thoughts.

With a little practice, you can learn to think as though your mind has a sieve. You can let your bad, gloomy thoughts go and think about cheerful, good things.

32

Praise the Lord!

Scripture: *He makes grass grow for the cattle, and plants for man to cultivate—bringing forth food from the earth. . . . How many are your works, O LORD! In wisdom you made them all. . . . Praise the LORD, O my soul. Praise the LORD* (Ps. 104:14, 24, 35).

Concept: Let's all praise God!

Object: A bouquet of flowers: wild, garden, or hothouse varieties

See what I brought with me today! *(Show the flowers.)* Aren't they beautiful? There are some daisies here, black-eyed Susans, some lupine, and even a little goldenrod. *(Finger through the bouquet and point out the different flowers. Keep the bouquet in your hands throughout the lesson and indicate it or gesture with it when appropriate.)*

Do flowers make you sad or happy? *(Pause for response.)* Happy, of course! Hardly anybody frowns when they look at flowers. Flowers are always pretty. Some seem so delicate. They're beautiful spots of color in the fields. You can't help but smile and feel happy when you see flowers like this.

Who made these flowers? *(Pause for response.)* God did! That's no secret. Of course, some people say that they just grow. But God told us that he made the earth and everything in it. God made all plants and flowers. I think he did a wonderful job when he created flowers like this.

Do you think God likes flowers? *(Pause for response.)* I do! I think God made these so pretty so that he could enjoy them and so that we could, too. They make us happy, and we can praise God for that.

That's why I brought these flowers today—so that we all could enjoy them and praise God who made them. *(Depending on the weather and what the children can see, add whatever is appropriate of the next sentences.)* We can look outside at the beautiful weather and be happy and praise God for that. We can look at all the green grass springing up and praise God for that. We can feel the warm breezes and praise God that spring is here. Look at the sunshine! Praise God for that. God gave us all sorts of beautiful things outside. They make us happy, and we can praise God for them.

How do we praise God? I'll tell you what I often do. When I see flowers like this, I say a little prayer. I usually say, "Thank you, God, for all the flowers. I praise you for them." I praise God with a little prayer.

Can you think of other ways to praise God? *(Pause for responses. Repeat the responses so that all can hear, and follow each response with an appropriate sentence. If responses are not forthcoming, use the paragraphs below.)*

Can we praise God with a little song? Of course! It doesn't have to be long and complicated. It can just be a happy little tune that you hum as you walk along. *(Demonstrate: "Hum-tee-dum-dum-dum. Praise God for these beautiful flowers.")*

Can we praise God with a little dance? Sure! We can even skip a little praise. We think, "What beautiful flowers God made!" as we skip along.

Can we praise God by talking about him? Yes! Say to someone, "God made all those wonderful flowers! Praise him!"

We can color pictures of the things God has made. That's praising God. We can write little poems about them. We can just sit silently and enjoy them, praising God in our hearts. And we can even shout in praise to God.

Don't these flowers (and the beautiful day, the grass, the sun, anything you want to add) make you just want to praise God? Let's praise God together. You may say a little prayer or hum a little tune, or even just sit quietly and praise God in your heart. Look at these gorgeous flowers. *(Hold them high.)* Let's praise God! *(Pause or lead a little response.)*

This is the time of year when you see lots of flowers. What can you do when you see them? *(Pause for response.)* That's right, PRAISE GOD!

33

A Cure for Your Cares

Scripture: *Cast all your anxiety on him because he cares for you* (1 Peter 5:7).

The prayer of a righteous man is powerful and effective (James 5:16).

Concept: Bring your cares to God in prayer.

Objects: Band-Aids, a bottle of aspirin, a cold remedy. (Put one of the Band-Aids on your finger.)

I cut myself yesterday, so I put on a Band-Aid. *(Show your finger with the Band-Aid.)* Besides keeping the blood from dripping all over, it does help a little bit. It keeps the cut clean and keeps the skin together so that it will heal well. How many of you have used Band-Aids? *(Show the Band-Aids.)* Good; then you know how they help.

When grownups get a headache, what do they do? *(Show the bottle of aspirin and pause for response.)* Sure, most of them will take an aspirin or two. That's often a good cure for a headache.

(Show the cold remedy.) I take this when I get a cold. It doesn't cure the cold, but it makes me feel a lot better. These pills are made especially to take for colds.

Nowadays we have lots of pills and other kinds of cures, don't we? We have pain pills, backache pills, drops for tired eyes, creams for sunburns, all sorts of cures for things that make us feel bad. If we follow directions and take them correctly, they can help make us feel better.

But those are all cures for our *bodies*. They're things we use to make us feel better on the outside, to make our bodies feel better.

There's no pill that we can take to make us feel better on the inside. When you feel sad and alone, is there a pill you can take? *(Shake your head and pause for response.)* If you are really worried about something, can you take a pill to make the worry go away? *(Shake your head and pause for response.)* If you're really scared of something, can you take a pill to make your fear go away? *(Shake your head and pause for response.)* No! These things *(indicate the pills and Band-Aids)* are for our bodies, not for our hearts and souls.

But there is a cure to make you feel better on the inside. There is something you can do to calm your fears and worries, to help your cares. Does anyone know what that is? *(Pause for response.)*

(You can have the children give their answers here and work toward the right one. Or you can give them the hint immediately.)

123

Here's a hint. *(Fold your hands and close your eyes as if you were praying.)* What can you do when you have cares and worries? *(Pause for response.)* Yes, you can pray to God. God loves you and has promised to help you.

The Bible says that you can give God all your worries, because he cares for you. The Bible also says that if you love Jesus your prayer will be effective. That means that your prayer *will* make a difference.

What kind of hurts can you have inside that you can pray about? *(Pause for response. Repeat each response so that all the children can hear. You may want to lead them with the following questions.)* If your best friend leaves you and you feel sad, can you pray about that? Of course. If a neighbor or a classmate teases you a lot, can you pray about that? Yes, God cares about that. If someone in your family is sick, can you pray about that? Please do. God says that your prayers make a difference. If you feel lonely, pray to God about that.

You can even say a quick prayer during the day, and God will hear you. He knows what you mean if you quickly say "Please help me, God," or "Be near me, Jesus."

The next time you need a cure for the outside you *(hold up the Band-Aids),* don't forget the inside you. When you put on that Band-Aid, you can also say a prayer *(show a Band-Aid as you speak):* "Dear God, I'm really lonely. Be near." God will hear you and help you.

Before you go to your seat, let's practice a bit by praying together. *(You may want to start your prayer here. Then use the inside hurts that were mentioned previously.)* Is there any inside hurt that you want to pray for? *(Pray for whatever the children mention.)*

Now you may go back to your seats. Know that God loves you and will hear your prayers.

34

Stick Close to God

Scripture: *But be very careful to . . . hold fast to him and to serve him with all your heart and all your soul* (Josh. 22:5).

Concept: We should stay close to God.

Objects: A good refrigerator magnet, something metal for the magnet to stick to (a metal spatula works), a small piece of paper with the above verse printed on it to give to each child

Can anyone tell me what this is? *(Show the magnet. Pause for and repeat the responses. If the children can't identify it, show how it sticks to the metal.)* That's right, it's a magnet. This is a pretty one that we usually keep on our refrigerator. *(Clamp it to the metal a few times to show how it works.)* When it's in place, we see this pattern (or picture, or fruit—whatever is on the magnet). It sticks to the refrigerator with this. *(Take it off and turn it around so the children can see the magnet.)* It's a magnet. It likes to stick to metal. I can't explain it. When it's near metal, it clamps itself on and sticks right there. *(Demonstrate as you speak.)* It doesn't slide around, it doesn't fall off, it stays right there. You have to pull it off.

How many of you have little things like this stuck on your refrigerator? *(Show the "pretty" side of the magnet and pause for response.)* Maybe some of your school work is there, or a picture that you drew. These magnets stick tightly enough to hold paper down. *(Demonstrate with one of the slips of paper.)* Lots of people stick things to their refrigerators with magnets. Let's see your hands once more. How many of you have magnets on your refrigerators? *(Raise your hand as you speak to encourage a like response.)*

Good! I thought you might have something like this. That's why I brought mine along. I want you to look at your magnet this week and have it remind you of something.

See the way it sticks to the metal? *(Demonstrate.)* That's the way it sticks to the refrigerator. You can do this with your magnet when you get home today. You can feel it sticking tight.

That's the way God wants you to stick tightly to him, just as your magnet is stuck tightly to your refrigerator. The Bible tells us to be very careful to hold fast, which means tightly, *(demonstrate with the magnet)* to God, so that we can serve him well. We should try to stay as close to God as this magnet does to a refrigerator.

(From now on, when you say "Stick close to," demonstrate by showing how the magnet is stuck.)

Nothing should be able to blow us away from God. *(Blow on the magnet.)* Nothing should be able to shake us loose from God. *(Shake the metal.)* God wants us to stick that closely to him.

What can help us stick close to God? Does it help if we pray? *(Pause for response.)* Of course! God hears us when we pray. He will help us stick close to him.

Will reading the Bible or listening while it's read help us stick close to God? *(Pause for response.)* It does. The Bible tells us how God loves us and wants us to love him.

What else helps us stick close to God? *(Pause for response and repeat the responses.)*

I've got something that will help you remember to stick close to God. *(Show the papers and read the verse.)* Each of you may have one.

When you go home today, ask Dad or Mom if you can put a magnet on the refrigerator. Then take this paper and stick it to the refrigerator under the magnet, like this. *(Demonstrate.)* Every time you see it, it can remind you to stick close to God.

(Pass out the papers as the children leave for their seats.)

35

God Is Real!

Scripture: *God is spirit* (John 4:24).

> *The wind blows wherever it pleases. You hear its sound, but you cannot tell where it comes from or where it is going. So it is with everyone born of the Spirit* (John 3:8).

Concept: God is invisible, but his work can be seen and felt.

Object: A down feather and a small piece of paper. (Practice blowing on this before you present the lesson to find the best way for you.)

Watch this. *(Blow on the feather.)* What moved that feather? *(Pause for response. You will have to coach the children with questions to elicit the right word.)* What did I make when I blew on it? A breeze? A breeze, or wind! That's right. I made the wind, but the wind moved the feather.

Watch this. *(Blow on the paper.)* What moved the paper? *(Pause for response.)* Yes, the wind again. I blew to make the wind. You saw the wind move the paper.

129

Can you try this? *(Fan yourself with your hand.)* Pretend that it's hot in here and you want to cool yourself. Can you do that? *(Pause while the children fan themselves.)* Now each of you made a little breeze. You made it windy right in front of your face. Did that breeze, that little wind, cool you? *(Nod your head as you speak and pause for response.)*

(Fan yourself again.) Can you see the breeze that I'm making? *(Shake your head and pause for response.)* Of course not! You can't see wind.

Fan yourself again. *(Let the children fan themselves.)* Can you feel the breeze that you're making? *(Nod and pause for response.)* Yes! You can't see wind, but you can feel it. You know that it's there.

(If the children can see through a window from where they are and there happens to be a strong breeze, ask them to look through the window.) What makes branches sway on trees? *(Demonstrate with your arms if the children are not looking outside, and pause for response.)* Yes, the wind! Can you see the wind? *(Pause for response.)* No! Can you see what the wind does? *(Pause for response.)* Yes, it sways the branches.

(Repeat the previous paragraph with "blows leaves off trees" if applicable. Then repeat it with "blows snow [or rain] sideways in a storm" if applicable.)

So, what moved this feather? *(Hold it up and pause for response.)* Yes, wind! *(Ask the review questions rather quickly to set up the rhythm of the response "Wind!")* What moved the paper? What cools your face? What makes branches sway? What blows leaves off trees? What blows snow in a storm?

Can we see wind? *(Pause for response.)* No! Can we see what it does? *(Blow the paper or feather and pause for response.)* Yes! Can we feel what it does? *(Fan yourself and pause for response.)* Yes!

We can't see wind, but we can see what it does and feel what it does.

In a way, God is like the wind. Can you see God? *(Shake your head and pause for response.)* No! We can't see God. God is invisible. Invisible means you can't see him, just like the wind.

Can we see what God does? *(Pause for response.)* Of course. Look outside and you'll see everything that God made. We can see what God does.

Sometimes we can see what God does in people's lives. Watch a generous person share with a friend. That's God working to make a person generous. Listen to someone tell you about Jesus. That's God working, telling you about Jesus. We can't see God, but we can see how God works.

Can you *feel* God working? When you really want to share your toys, when you really love your family, when you really try to be good, is that God working in you? *(Nod your head and pause for response.)* Yes, that's God working. So we can *feel* God work.

The only problem is that we can't see God. We can see what God does and we can feel what God does. But like the wind, God is invisible; we can't see him.

But the wind can help remind you that God is real and God is here. When you see the tree branches moving or leaves coming off the trees or rain coming down sideways, you know that the wind is at work. When you feel a strong breeze, you know that it's windy. Look hard for the wind. You won't see it. But it can remind you of God. You can't see God, but he is real.

36

Different Gifts

Scripture: *There are different kinds of gifts, but the same Spirit. There are different kinds of service, but the same Lord* (1 Cor. 12:4–5).

Concept: God has given each one of us a gift to use in his service.

Objects: Gift-wrapped boxes and envelopes. (Make a few very easy to open. Inside each of those place a slip of paper with the word for a gift, such as *healing, teaching, friendliness, generosity*, written on it.)

I have a whole bunch of gifts with me today. *(Show the gifts.)*

Let's talk about gifts for a minute before we open some.

When someone gives you a gift, do you pay for it, or is it free? *(Pause for response.)* Of course, it's free. That's what makes it a gift. If you pay for something or work to earn it, it isn't a gift; it's something you earned. A gift is something that you get free. You don't deserve a gift; you just get it.

Do you give yourself a gift, or does someone give it to you? *(Pause for response.)* That's right, someone gives it to you, free. They want to give you something, so they give you a gift.

Does a gift always have to be wrapped up and solid, like these? *(Hold up one of the gifts.)* Or can someone give you a gift you can't even see? If you're supposed to put away your toys and someone else does it for you, is that a gift? *(Nod your head and pause for response.)* I'd call that a gift. They're using their time to do you a favor. They give you a gift of time. Or, if you're feeling lonely and a friend comes to play with you, is that a gift? *(Nod and pause for response.)* I think so. That person gives you the gift of friendship just when you need it.

So, do all gifts have to be solid and wrapped like these? *(Shake your head and pause for response.)* No! There are all sorts of gifts people can give each other.

In fact, there are all sorts of gifts that God has given to people. These are the kinds of gifts you can't see.

Since you can't see them, I wrote some of them down and hid them in these packages. Let's see what we have.

(Unwrap a gift and take out the paper.) This says "healing." God gives some people the gift of healing. Do you like to visit sick people and do things to make them feel better? *(Look around and pause for response.)* Not everybody does. If you do, maybe you have the gift of healing. God made you able to visit sick people so that you can help them.

(Unwrap another gift and take out the paper.) This says "teaching." God gives some people the gift of

teaching. Do you catch on to things real fast and like to explain them to others? *(Look around and pause for response.)* Not everybody does. Maybe God gave you the gift of teaching. You can teach others about God.

(Unwrap one more gift.) This says "friendliness." Do you like to talk to people and have lots of friends? *(Look around and pause for response.)* Then God gave you the gift of friendliness. You can welcome strangers to our church or new kids to your school or neighborhood.

There are lots of these gifts left, too many to open now. God has given each one of us a special gift that we can use for him.

You have your gift from God already, but it may be invisible. Maybe you can't see it. You have to discover what it is.

This is the way you discover it: You have to think about yourself—what you like and what you can do very well—to discover that as being your gift from God. He has given you a way to be very special; that's his gift to you. And when you discover it and know what it is, think about how you can use it for him. That's your gift back to God.

And the next time you open a gift like this *(indicate one of the packages)*, you can think about the invisible gift that God has given to you.

37

Toddling with God

Scripture: *If the LORD delights in a man's way, he makes his steps firm; though he stumble, he will not fall, for the LORD upholds him with his hand* (Ps. 37:23–24).

Concept: God will help us walk with him.

Objects:

1. A toddler and her parent from your congregation, or

2. A cane, crutch, walker, or walking stick (This lesson can be done two ways. Material in option 1 is for use with the toddler. Material in option 2 is for use with the other objects. Other material can be used with either.)

Option 1

(<u>Name of toddler</u>) is just learning how to walk. She's having a little trouble yet, so Dad has to help. See how well she is doing.

(Have the parent hold the hands of the toddler as she walks where the other children can see her.) She probably can take some steps alone but can't go very far without help. *(Have the parent let the toddler try walking*

alone but come to her rescue when she falls. Then parent and toddler can go back to their seats.) But Dad is right there to help and hold her up when she stumbles.

Option 2

(Show the children the cane, crutch, or whatever.) Can anyone tell me what this is? *(Pause for response.)* That's right, it's a cane. It's something nice and sturdy to help me walk.

Now, usually we don't have trouble walking all by ourselves, do we? But once in a while we may need help. Maybe we sprain an ankle or we break a leg or maybe just walk in a really bumpy place. Then a cane keeps us from falling.

(Demonstrate with the cane.) You're OK for a while, but you hit a rough spot or your leg is too weak. Then you lean on the cane. It's nice and sturdy. You can put all your weight on it and it won't break. It's here to help you in case you stumble.

Continue Lesson

We usually don't need help when we walk, do we? *(Shake your head and pause for response.)* No! Usually we do just fine, all by ourselves. (1. We're not toddlers.) (2. We don't need canes.)

Do you know what we are (or do) in God's eyes? (1. We're all toddlers.) (2. We all have trouble walking.) We often stumble and fall.

137

I don't mean that we stumble when we're walking, like this. *(Walk a few steps.)* I mean that we stumble when we're walking with God; we stumble in the way we live. Let me explain that.

God wants us to act lovingly to people, right? So, if we forget to do that to someone, that's a little stumble. It's not walking as God wants us to.

God wants us always to be honest, right? So, if we tell a lie, that's a stumble. We're making a mistake in our walk with God.

God loves a cheerful giver, right? So if we're stingy, that's a little stumble.

I think we all stumble at times. We don't live just the way God wants us to. We don't stay close to God all the time. (1. We're like toddlers when we walk with God.) (2. We stumble when life gets rough and we need a cane.) None of us can walk the way God wants us to without help.

Who's going to help us? *(Pause for response.)* Of course, God says that he will help us. The Bible says that if we stumble we will not fall, for God will hold us up with his hand. That means that God will help us walk well with him. God will help us avoid those little stumbles like telling lies or being stingy.

Option 1

God will help us just as (toddler's name) Dad helped her. God will stay near to us and help us in what we do. God won't let us fall. If we stumble, he will hold us up with his hand.

Option 2

God will help us just as this cane helps people who have trouble walking. God is always near us and is strong. If we stumble *(demonstrate with the cane)*, we can lean on him, and he will not let us fall.

Continue Lesson

You can go back to your seats now. I'm sure you won't stumble, because you've got good legs and feet. But through the week, if you feel like you're going to stumble that other way—if you have trouble living the way God wants you to—think about (1. <u>Toddler's name</u>) (2. this cane), and remember that God will help you walk with him.

38

Caring for Creation

Scripture: *The earth is the LORD's, and every-thing in it, the world, and all who live in it* (Ps. 24:1).

Concept: All of creation belongs to the Lord. We should treat it with care.

Objects: Jars, each containing one of the fol-lowing: daddy longlegs, ant, spider, small beetle, earthworm. (How long or short this lesson is depends on the creatures you use. You can use one, a combination, or all of them. Some facts are given about each for your convenience. Make sure you provide whatever you catch with some comfort: some slightly moist soil, leaves, grass, and air holes in the lid.)

I brought a few living things with me today, so we can talk about how neat they are. *(Show a few jars.)* When we look at any one of these we can see that God made everything exactly right when he cre-ated it.

(Hold a jar close to someone near you.) What's in this jar? *(Pause for response.)* A daddy longlegs!

Daddy longlegs is really a gentle little thing. It doesn't chase and catch bugs. It usually eats dead stuff, like dead bugs and leaves and rotten berries. It can't hurt you. It has no fangs or poison in its body. It doesn't need fangs and poison to eat dead stuff. So God didn't give it fangs.

If I let it out of the jar *(shake it onto the floor),* it probably wouldn't go very far. It would just walk around looking for something to eat.

Sometimes, when people see a daddy longlegs inside the house, they're scared of it, so they kill it for no reason at all. Better to put it back into the jar and put it outside where it belongs. *(Put it back into the jar, gently. If you don't want to handle it or other critters, scoop it up onto a small piece of paper.)*

(Hold the jar up again for all to see.) After all, this little creature is alive. Who made it and gave it life? *(Pause for response.)* God did! Can we make a living daddy longlegs? *(Pause for response.)* Of course not. We can't replace this one, so we'll let it live outside where it belongs.

(Continue in this manner with the other creatures. Point out a few "neat" facts. If the creature is slow moving, you can let it go free so the children get a feel for the thing out of its place. Ask what happens when it wanders into the house or out of its place. Point out that it's alive, it belongs to God, and we can't make life. So it's better to let it live in its place.)

Facts

Ants work together socially. One cannot survive alone away from the colony. *(Mention putting it back exactly where it was found.)* They "speak" to each other by means of chemicals. They can "tell" each other when there is trouble in their ant city, when everything is OK, and even whom to follow to find food. They often are responsible for aerating soil, and some keep certain insects in check.

Spiders keep the insect population in check. There are over thirty thousand different kinds of spiders. Some females take care of their young. Every spider has at least two hundred silk glands within its body; some have eight hundred silk glands.

There are more types of *beetles* than any other creature on the earth. Their hard outer shells are made like layers of ribbed package tape set at angles to prevent ripping. Those two wings over their backs are used only to protect a pair of more delicate wings beneath them. Their antennae are usually very sensitive and can "smell" chemicals we are unaware of. Ladybugs and lightning bugs also are beetles.

Earthworms are most often responsible for aerating the soil and enriching it. They digest tiny bits of organic material found in soils. Although they have no eyes, they respond to light and are very chemically sensitive. They often can grow new tails. They can live to be several years old, if they are careful. Certain worms grow to be several feet long. Without earthworms our soil would be barely tillable.

Continue Lesson

By now you probably have the idea. All of these creatures are alive. Can we make something that's alive? *(Pause for response.)* No, we can't. Only God can make life. God gave all these creatures life.

None of these little creatures *(indicate the jars)* belong to us, do they? To whom do they belong? *(Pause for response.)* That's right, they belong to God.

The Bible tells us that the earth is the Lord's and everything in it, the world and all who live in it. That includes these little creatures. God made them, and they're his.

So how should we treat this life that God made? Can we do anything we want with it, or should we take care of it? *(Pause for response.)* Of course! We should take care of it. We can't make life, we can only appreciate it. Only God can make life.

The earth is the Lord's and everything in it—even daddy longlegs, ants, spiders, beetles, and worms! When we see these things we can have lots of fun watching them. And then we can remember that God made them and they belong to God. We should be very gentle with them and take good care of them.

39

Gone and Forgotten

Scripture: *For I will forgive their wickedness and will remember their sins no more* (Heb. 8:12).

Concept: If you believe in Jesus, God will forget your sins.

Objects: A piece of paper with approximately ten letters neatly printed on it in pencil, a good eraser, a hard surface on which to lay paper and erase it

Can any of you read the letters of the alphabet? *(Pause for response and choose one likely candidate. Give that child the paper.)* I'd like you to read some of these letters for me, slowly and loudly. *(Repeat each letter after the child reads it. Do approximately five letters, then take the paper from the child.)* Thank you.

There are more letters on that paper. They don't spell anything. They're just a bunch of letters. *(Speak a few more sentences if the child read fewer letters. The idea is to talk a bit so that the children forget the letters.)*

I wanted to try something with you and those letters. Can you remember them? Who can remember all of the letters in the order that (the child's name)

read them. Who can remember? *(Pause and let a few children try.)* Some of you did very well, but it's difficult, isn't it? You only heard them once.

Would you remember if I showed you the paper again? *(Show the letters on the paper.)* If you forgot them, you could always read them again, couldn't you?

There are some other letters on the paper. I want you to try to remember them. But I have to do something to the paper first. *(Take out the eraser and erase all of the letters. Continue to speak as you erase.)*

I know that you're going to say this isn't fair. We told you a few letters and asked you to remember them. That was hard enough. Most of you forgot them. Now I'm going to ask you to remember the letters that I'm erasing right now. You won't even see them. How can you remember them? You'll never know them. Let's give it a try.

(Show the erased paper.) There you are! Can you remember the new letters? Can you even remember the letters that we did first? Have you forgotten them all? They're all gone; we'll never remember them.

How did I get rid of them? *(Hold up the eraser and pause for response.)* That's right, I used an eraser. I took this handy little eraser and rubbed all the marks right off the page. It almost looks like they were never there. *(Show them the erased paper again.)* This eraser is a neat little gadget. It gets rid of our mistakes or things we don't want on the paper.

But it can only get rid of writing mistakes, can't it? Do you know there are bigger mistakes that we all make, that this eraser can't get rid of? If we're naughty or say something nasty, that's a big mistake, isn't it? God doesn't like that; he calls it a sin. And we can't erase that. When it's done, it's done. *(Write "mistake" or "sin" on the paper, same side as your erasures, and show it to the children.)* An eraser can't make a real sin disappear.

But there is someone who is like an eraser for our sins. Who is that? *(Pause for response.)* Jesus! You're right! The Bible tells us that if we believe in Jesus, God will forget our sins.

(Hold up the eraser.) Jesus acts just like this eraser. *(Erase as you speak.)* Because Jesus died for our sins, they are all erased. God promised that he will forget them, just as you forgot the letters. *(Hold up the erased sheet of paper.)*

But Jesus erases our sins much better than I erased. He takes every trace of them away. God really does forget all our sins because of Jesus. He sees us as if we are like this. *(Hold up the clean side of the paper.)* All our sins are forgiven.

All of us make mistakes and use erasers *(hold up the eraser)* once in a while. When you use an eraser like this you can think of Jesus. He erases all of our sins.

40

God's Dandelions

Scripture: *And my God will meet all your needs according to his glorious riches in Christ Jesus* (Phil. 4:19).

Concept: God will give you everything you need.

Objects: A bouquet of dandelions along with a few dandelion leaves and one gone to seed—save some of the "parachutes" if they fall off. (You can do this lesson with all or any one of these dandelion parts.) If you live in an area where dandelions do not grow, use another local hardy weed.

I picked a bouquet of dandelions to show you today, because I think that they're really interesting. God gave dandelions everything that they need to grow well wherever they grow.

Look closely at these flowers. *(Hold the flowers close to the children.)* Each of these flowers *(pick one blossom from the bouquet and hold it up)* is really hundreds of flowers bunched together.

What we think are little petals *(pick off one "petal" and hold it up)* are really complete flowers. This little

147

flower-that-looks-like-a-petal can make a perfect seed, just as any flower can. I think that God wants to be sure this dandelion makes seeds. That's really what flowers are for.

See this stem? *(Hold up one flower with a longish stem and point to the stem.)* This is specially made to help the dandelion live through lots of wind and rain. It's hollow inside. *(Let the children try to see the inside of the stem.)* When the wind blows, this hollow stem bends really easily. In fact, the stems bend right here in my hand. Some flower stems break when you bend them, but not the dandelion. It can bend almost all the way down and still live.

See this leaf? *(Hold at least one leaf up for everyone to see.)* See the jagged edges and the track down the center? *(Point them out.)* God put that there so that the leaf could collect water and send it right down to the root. *(Demonstrate the path for water down the center of the leaf to the taproot.)*

And the root of a dandelion is really long and strong. That's why I didn't bring any to show you. It's hard to dig up a whole dandelion root. I think God knew that people would keep trying to dig up dandelions. He gave them long strong roots to hold them in place.

Here's one that has made seed already. *(Show the puffy seedhead.)* Why, do you think, did God make these seeds like little parachutes? *(Pick off one seed with its "parachute" and let it float on the air.)* That's right, so that the seeds could float all over the place.

And if you could look at the seed really closely, you'd see something else. It has little ridges on it, just like a screw. When the seed lands, it can work its way into the ground and plant itself! *(Illustrate with a circular motion going down with one finger.)*

These dandelions are really wonderful. God gave them everything they need to grow well.

I wanted to show you these because we all see many dandelions, don't we? And now, when you see a dandelion, you can think of something else.

Remember I said—and I showed you—that God gave them everything they need to grow well? That can help remind you that God can and does give you his children everything you need to live and to grow as Christians.

God said that he will meet all our needs. Maybe we need a little patience one day. Or another day we may need some cheer. Or we may need something as simple and necessary as food. Or we may need help in solving a problem. God will meet all our needs. He said so.

Can you think of some things you need to live well and to be a good Christian? *(Pause for response; repeat the responses for everyone to hear. If they do not respond, ask the following questions.)* Do you need enough food? Do you need clothes? Do you need to stay healthy? Do you need help to be generous? Do you need to be more loving? Do you need to talk about Jesus to a friend?

You can always ask God to help you with your needs. God said that he will supply all your needs.

Just look at the dandelions and think about how God gave them everything they need. God loves you much more than dandelions. He will meet all your needs.

41

God's Love Forever . . . and Ever . . . and Ever

Scripture: *But you remain the same, and your years will never end* (Ps. 102:27).

Concept: God will always be God and he will always love us.

Objects: Any or all of the following: a flashlight with a dead battery, a prescription drug or a bottle of aspirin with an expiration date, a container of food with an expiration date printed on it, a dead flower or plant part

Something's wrong with this flashlight. *(Try to switch it on a few times.)* It doesn't want to go on. Does anyone have an idea of what's wrong? *(Pause for response. Repeat the responses until you receive the correct one.)* I think that's it. I think one of the batteries is dead. *(Open the flashlight and show the batteries.)* These batteries make the flashlight work. If one of them is worn out or dead, the flashlight simply won't work, will it? Batteries do wear out; they don't last forever. Then we have to recharge them or buy new batteries. The old one simply is no good.

(Show the prescription drug or aspirin.) These wear out, too. At least they don't work very well after a certain date. That date is printed right here. It says expiration date—that's when it's worn out—October 1995 (or whatever it is). If I use these aspirin after 1995, after they're old, will they work well? *(Pause for response.)* Maybe and maybe not. Can I trust these aspirin after a certain date? *(Pause for response.)* I don't know. I probably wouldn't trust them to be good.

Here's something I wouldn't trust after it's old. *(Show the food.)* This is a carton of yogurt, and there's a date on it, too. It says *(read the whole expiration date, including the "Do not use" or "Sell before").* What might happen if I use this long after that date? *(Pause for response.)* I might get sick. Maybe this yogurt (or whatever) goes bad or spoils when it gets old. Would you trust this yogurt when it's old? *(Pause for response.)* I don't think I would.

Everything that we make gets old. It turns bad or spoils or wears out, doesn't it? Not everything comes stamped with dates telling us when it's old, but we know that it won't last forever.

Even the things that God created get old or wear out. What, do you suppose, happened to this flower (or plant)? *(Pause for response.)* Sure, this became old, too. It was beautiful in its day, but it got old and died. It probably served its purpose and then wore out the way plants wear out. It simply won't last forever.

Nothing lasts forever, does it? You can name anything on this earth, and I can say, "That will get old" or "That will wear out." Nothing lasts forever.

152

Or does it? Is there one thing or one person that can last forever? *(Pause for response.)* That's right! God lasts forever. He's the only thing or person that will never get old, never go bad, and never wear out. The Bible tells us that God will always remain the same and his years will never end.

That's very hard for us to understand. We understand things that do wear out *(show the flashlight)* or get old *(the aspirin)* or spoil *(the food)* or simply die *(the flower)*. But that will never happen to God. God will always be here and he will always be the same God.

Although that's hard to understand, that also makes me feel very good. Do you know why? Because the Bible says that God loves us and watches over us and keeps us in his care. Then the Bible says that God will always remain the same.

Will God ever stop loving us? *(Pause for response.)* No! Will God ever stop thinking about us? *(Pause for response.)* No! Will God ever stop caring for us? *(Pause for response.)* No! God's love will be with us forever and ever and ever.

You may get frustrated when a battery dies *(show the flashlight)*, or when some food spoils *(show the yogurt)*. You may not like to see a pretty flower die. *(Show the flower.)* But each one of these can remind you that God will live forever and he won't change. God will love you forever and ever and ever.

42

Grumbles and Grudges

Scripture: *Do not seek revenge or bear a grudge against one of your people, but love your neighbor as yourself. I am the LORD* (Lev. 19:18).

Don't grumble against each other, brothers, or you will be judged (James 5:9).

Concept: We should not grumble or bear grudges.

Objects: A doormat, a pair of muddy shoes

How many of you have a doormat like this or a little different outside a door at home? *(Show the doormat. Pause for response.)* Who can tell me what this is for? *(Raise your hand as you ask the question to encourage a similar response. If a response is not forthcoming, hold up a muddy shoe as a hint.)* That's right. This is for wiping your feet before you go into the house. If you have mud on your shoes like this *(show the bottom of a muddy shoe)* you can wipe it on the mat. *(Wipe the shoe on the mat and show the cleaned shoe.)* Then you go into the house with clean feet. You leave the dirt outside on the mat. *(Show the dirt on the mat if you can.)*

How many of you have heard this: "Wipe your feet"? *(Say it as if you're calling out to a child.)* Probably all of you have heard that at some time. No one likes dirt tracked into the house. So your parents tell you to wipe the dirt off your feet.

God wants us to wipe the dirt off, too. But God doesn't talk about wiping our feet. He wants us to get what's inside of us clean. He wants us to have nice clean hearts and souls. To do that, God says that we should have no grumbles and grudges.

I'll explain that in a minute. But first I want to be sure you can say that. Please say "grumbles and grudges" with me. Ready? Grumbles and grudges. Say it again. Grumbles and grudges. One more time, nice and loudly. Grumbles and grudges.

A grumble is to say something like this. *(Say it in a grumbly tone of voice.)* I don't want to play with Johnny. I always have to play with Johnny. I hate playing with Johnny. Why do I have to play with Johnny? Does that sound familiar? You grumble when you don't like something or someone. You rumble and mutter about him. That's grumbling. That's like dirt in your heart. *(Show dirt on the other shoe.)*

The Bible tells us not to grumble. Don't have any grumbles. Stop grumbling. *(Wipe the shoe a bit on the mat.)*

A grudge is to keep on being angry with someone because he did something. And you'll never forget it. Johnny rode my new bike and scratched it. I'll never let him ride it again. I'll never play with

Johnny, because he scratched my bike. I don't like Johnny; he scratched my bike! That's a grudge. You'll never like Johnny because he happened to scratch your bike once. That's like dirt in your heart. *(Show dirt on a shoe, if there still is some.)*

The Bible tells us not to hold a grudge. Forget about the scratch on the bike. Instead, God says, we should love each other. Don't hold that grudge. Show Johnny some love. Wipe that dirt out of your heart. *(Wipe the shoe on the mat.)*

No grumbles *(wipe a shoe on the mat)* or grudges *(wipe the other shoe on the mat. Repeat the sentence and action at least once more.)*

We really have to try to get rid of our grumbles and grudges. Sometimes we forget and we grumble again or hold a grudge. That's why I brought along this doormat. *(Hold up the mat.)* The one that you have at home can remind you of grumbles and grudges.

If someone tells you to wipe your feet, you can even say "grumbles and grudges" to remind yourself. Like this *(wipe the shoes on the mat while you say it in rhythm with the wiping):* grumbles and grudges, grumbles and grudges.

Try it once more with me. *(Say the next as if you are calling to a child.)* Wipe your feet! Grumbles and grudges, grumbles and grudges *(while wiping the shoes).*

That can remind you that God tells you not to grumble or hold a grudge. Wipe them right off your heart.

43

In Case of Fire *(Missions Sunday)*

Scripture: *How, then, can they call on the one they have not believed in? And how can they believe in the one of whom they have not heard? And how can they hear without some-one preaching to them* (Rom. 10:14)?

Concept: People who have not heard of Jesus need someone to tell them.

Objects: A fire extinguisher and a Bible

Who can tell me what this is? *(Hold up the fire extinguisher so that everyone can see it. Pause for response.)* That's right, it's a fire extinguisher. What can we do with it? *(Pause for response.)* Yes, we put out fires with it. This *(hold it up high)* can save your life.

Imagine, just for a minute, that you are trapped in a fire. *(It's better to be general than to specify the children's house or bedrooms, because you don't want recall on this part.)* Here's your fire extinguisher. *(Thrust the extinguisher out towards them.)* It can save your life. What are you going to do?

(If you're bold and have enough time, you may want to press this point so that the children themselves discover the next point: "How do you use this? What do you do first? Is there a button to press?" etc.)

Come to think of it, *I* don't even know how to use this thing. Usually directions are printed right on a fire extinguisher. *(Look it over and read a few of the directions aloud.)* Thank goodness for directions! If they weren't printed here, this fire extinguisher would do me no good.

Could you read all these directions? There are some big words in here; maybe you haven't learned them yet. Could you understand all of this? *(Pause for response.)* Maybe not. Then, if you had a fire and even had this extinguisher, would it do you any good? *(Shake your head to elicit the right response.)* Probably not. You'd need someone to explain the directions to you. Then you might be able to use it to put out the fire.

Here we have something that could save your life. *(Hold up the fire extinguisher.)* But someone caught in a fire without it *(put it behind your back)* could die. Even if you have it *(bring it to where the children can see it)* but don't know how to use it, you're still in trouble. You must have and know how to use this lifesaver.

We have another lifesaver here. *(Hold up the Bible.)* This is much more important than a fire extinguisher, isn't it? This saves your life forever. If you believe the Bible, you can have eternal life.

But what if you don't have a Bible or don't even know about a Bible? *(Put the Bible behind your back.)* It can't do you any good then, can it?

There are people who don't have Bibles. Some don't even know about the Bible or what the Bible says. How can you believe in Jesus if you've never heard about him? You can't, can you?

That's like being in a burning room without a fire extinguisher. You don't even know that there's help.

What can we do about people who have no Bibles or don't even know about the Bible? *(Pause for response.)* That's right. We can send them Bibles. We can give money to help them buy Bibles.

Some people have Bibles but don't really understand what's written in them, or they don't believe what's written. That's like having a fire extinguisher but not knowing how to use it. What can we do about that? *(Pause for response.)* Yes! We can go to those people and help them read the Bible. We can tell them about Jesus. We can pray that they will believe the Bible. And if we can't go to help them, we can help other people to go. And we can pray for those who go to help people understand the Bible.

(Hold up the fire extinguisher.) It's always a good idea to have one of these around the house. Maybe you can get an adult to show you how to use it. Someday it could save your life.

But this fire extinguisher *(hold up the Bible)* is much, much more important. This saves people for eternal life. We should make sure that everyone in the whole world has, knows how to use, and believes this.

Why We Say No

Scripture: *Do you not know that your body is a temple of the Holy Spirit, who is in you, whom you have received from God? You are not your own; you were bought at a price. Therefore honor God with your body* (1 Cor. 6:19–20).

Concept: Our bodies belong to God; we should treat them with respect.

Objects: A wastebasket with some trash (used paper, etc.) and some garbage (old food, etc.) in it, cigarettes, pills

(As the children are seating themselves, take some of the trash from the wastebasket and throw it on the floor.)

$\mathbf{D}$o you like having all this trash on the floor? *(Shake your head as you ask the question and pause for response.)* Of course not! Neither do I. Do you ever throw trash on the floor at home or church? *(Pause for response.)* No!

Why don't we throw trash around the house or around church? *(Pause for response. Repeat all responses.)* You're right. We just don't do it. *(Pick up the trash and throw it into the wastebasket.)*

(Take some of the garbage and lay it on the floor. Continue to speak as you do so.) This is even worse, I think, so I'll do it just for a minute. See this icky garbage? Do you ever do this? Do you ever throw garbage around the church, or around your house? *(Pause for response.)* Of course not! Garbage is almost worse than the trash. This can stain the carpet, stink, and ruin some things that it's on. *(Pick up the garbage and put it back into the wastebasket. Wipe up any spill.)*

(Show the children the cigarettes.) These are cigarettes. We've heard lots of warnings that they can make you very sick. When you grow up, should you smoke these? *(Pause for response.)* Of course not! Why do something that will make you sick? Cigarette smoke in your body is like that trash on the floor. At least, it's something that doesn't belong there. It's almost like that garbage on the floor. It can start to ruin parts of your body.

(Hold the cigarettes over the wastebasket.) What should we do with these things? *(Pause for response.)* Yes! It's best just to throw them away; don't even touch them.

(Show the children the pills.) Here's a bunch of drugs. I don't really know what they are. Maybe a doctor told someone else to take them. But I'm not sick. Should I take them? Should I put them into my body? *(Pause for response.)* No! Too many drugs could ruin my body. What should I do with these drugs? *(Pause for response.)* That's right; I should throw them away. *(Throw them into the wastebasket.)*

Taking drugs that aren't meant for me, or taking pills when I'm not sick is like throwing trash and garbage around church or your house. We don't do it. That's not good; it can ruin things. This stuff belongs in a wastebasket.

Lots of people will tell you that cigarettes and drugs and other things are not good for you. Lots of people will tell you to throw them away or not touch them in the first place. And that's very good advice. Why throw garbage around church? Why do things that are bad for your body? It doesn't make sense to do something that's bad for you, does it? *(Shake your head and pause for response.)* That's why lots of people tell you not to do those things.

But we have another reason for being good to our bodies. We should never do dangerous things to our bodies, because God told us not to. God said that our bodies belong to him. God lives in us. Our bodies are like his house. We don't own our bodies; God does. And he told us to treat our bodies with respect—to honor him with our bodies.

As you grow up, lots of people are going to tell you not to smoke or do drugs or other dangerous things. That's good advice. That's like saying not to throw garbage around the house.

And then they'll say that those things are bad for you. That's so true. Don't ever forget that. These things *(indicate the cigarettes and drugs)* belong in the trash can, not your bodies.

We know that there's another, very important reason why we shouldn't pollute our bodies with these things. Why is that? *(Pause for response.)* Yes! We belong to God. Our bodies are his. We should always treat them with respect.

As you go back to your seats, look at the church. It looks good, doesn't it? No trash or garbage on the floor. We should be even more careful with our bodies. Never trash them.

45

Pruned for Our Good

Scripture: *And we know that in all things God works for the good of those who love him* (Rom. 8:28).

Concept: Because God is in control, everything that happens to us is for our good.

Object: An unpruned houseplant. (It should have a few dead leaves, two cracked stems, and perhaps a dying flower.)

This plant looks a bit scraggly, doesn't it? *(Show the plant.)* I haven't worked with it lately. I thought I could do it now so you can see what happens. We're going to take these funny things off and make the plant good again.

(Do any or all of the pruning below.)

(Take off the dead leaves.) These have served their purpose. They're only clogging up the plant now, so let's take them off.

This flower has seen better days. *(Point out the flower.)* It was pretty when it was alive, but it's almost dead now. It's just sapping strength out of the plant.

Let's take it off. Even if it's not quite done blossoming, the plant would be better off without it. *(Pinch off the flower.)*

Looks like there was a minor accident here. *(Point out the cracked stem.)* This stem might have grown big and strong, but something happened. It's not going to do the plant much good the way it is. Since it's broken anyway, let's take it off. *(Pinch off the shoot.)* That's better.

Option 1

This plant is really a little bushy. I'd rather have it grow straight and tall. Do you know how we do that? We simply take off some of these stems. We'll take off a few shorter ones and let the tall ones stand. Then all the plant's energy will go into growing those tall stems. I know these are good stems, but the plant will be better yet without them. Sorry, stems. *(Wince a little as you take them off.)* It almost hurts me to take off a living stem, but I know it's better for the plant.

Option 2

This plant is really quite tall and leggy. I'd like it to grow a little more bushy. Do you know how we do that? I'll pinch the top off some of these stems. *(Pinch and wince as you speak.)* These should stop growing now, and the plant will bush out. It almost hurts me to pinch the top off a living stem, but I know that it's better for the plant.

Continue Lesson

(Prune as you talk.) Pretend for a minute that the plant can think the way you and I think. How, do you suppose, it would feel about this pruning that I'm doing? Would it like to be poked and have stems torn from it? *(Pause for response.)* Probably not!

If this plant had feelings like ours, tearing a stem from it would hurt, wouldn't it? *(Pause for response.)* It certainly wouldn't feel good.

And if this plant could think, it would probably wonder what in the world I'm doing to it. I'd have to explain that all these horrible things that are happening are really for its own good. It will be a better plant in the end. This may hurt, but I know the plant will be better because of this pruning.

In a way, you and I are like this plant to God. Not really, because we can think and we can talk to God. We can ask God what's going on. But we can't see the future as God can. And we don't know if bad things that happen are going to turn out to be good.

Bad things do happen sometimes, don't they? Maybe a best friend moves away. Or a parent moves away. Or someone we know dies. We can't say that these things are good, can we? *(Shake your head and pause for response.)* No! But they happen anyway.

That's sort of like the stem that cracked on this plant. *(Show the other cracked stem.)* That wasn't a good thing. But I turned it into a good thing for the plant, didn't I?

The Bible tells us that God will turn the bad things that happen to us into good, if we love God.

God loves us and wants only good for us. So he takes these bad things and turns them into our good. *(Take off the other cracked stem.)* Maybe we can't see now how it can be good. When it happens, all we know is that it hurts and it seems bad. But God said that he would turn it to our good, so we trust him.

Maybe sometimes God has things happen to us that we think are bad. That's sort of like taking off a dead leaf, isn't it? God knows what he's doing is best for us in the end. All we know is that we don't like it. But we can't see the future, and God can. God tells us it is for our good. So we trust him.

(Hold up your pruned plant.) There we are. Isn't that a lot better? Now all the junk is gone and the plant will be able to grow strong and healthy. It's just like us and the things that hurt. If we love God, he will help us and turn it all to our good, so that we can be strong and healthy Christians.

46

Avoid It!

Scripture: *Avoid every kind of evil* (1 Thess. 5:22).

Concept: We should avoid all evil.

Object: A housefly in a jar

Can you see what's in here? *(Show the children the fly.)* It's a housefly that I caught yesterday. It was inside my house. I'm going to let it go outside. I don't want a fly in my house. I suppose you wouldn't, either.

Why don't we want flies in our houses? *(Pause for response.)* That's right, they're dirty. They bring germs into the house.

Flies belong outside. They help clean up messes in nature. They were created to live and breed in dirty, yucky places. Somehow, they can live with all that dirt and filth. But we can't. We don't want those yucky germs near us, so we make sure that flies stay outside.

Would you like me to open this jar and let the fly loose in here? *(Pause for response.)* Probably not, and I won't let it go here. If there were a fly in here and it came and sat on you, what would you do? *(Gesture as if to brush a fly away from you and pause for response.)* That's right, you'd brush it off, wouldn't you? No one wants germs near them, so they brush away the flies to avoid the germs.

Even when you're outside where flies live, do you let them sit on you? *(Pause for response.)* Of course not. When you see a bunch of flies swarming around some yucky garbage, do you poke around in it and let the flies crawl all over you? *(Pause for response.)* No! Too many germs, too much yucky stuff. There are some things that you avoid, or stay away from, and that you brush away if they come too near. A fly is one of those things.

There's something else that we all should stay away from, even more than we avoid a germy fly. The Bible tells us that we should avoid evil. Evil things are bad things. God says that we should avoid bad things. We should stay away from bad things the way we stay away from dirty flies. And if we see and hear bad things, we should brush them away the way we brush off a fly.

What, do you think, are bad things that we can avoid or brush off? *(Pause for response. Prompt the children with a few questions. Every time you mention something to avoid, shoo it away or brush it off, as you would a fly.)* What about dirty, nasty language? Does God want us to use dirty, nasty language? Does God like it when we say bad things? We should avoid dirty, nasty language. How about being mean to our friends? Should we avoid that? When we feel mean, we should brush that meanness away.

Sometimes there are TV programs that Mom and Dad don't want us to watch. Should we try to sneak them? No! They may be bad for us. Stay away from them. Are there places that Dad and Mom don't want you to go? Do they take you to dangerous places? Of course not! There are certain places and things we avoid, because they're not good for us. They're bad, and we should avoid all evil.

Now, we don't like to talk about all bad things, do we? We can concentrate on good things. We can talk nicely, be good to our friends, love and obey our parents, and show our love to God. That's kind of like picking a nice bouquet of flowers when we are outside, or looking at butterflies. That helps us avoid the dirty things in life *(show the fly)* and stay away *(gesture as if shooing it away)* from evil.

You probably see flies like this *(hold up the jar)* every day. You probably always avoid them. Now they can help remind you to avoid bad things in your life, too.

47

Three-in-One *(Trinity)*

Scripture: *In the name of the Father and of the Son and of the Holy Spirit* (Matt. 28:19).

Concept: God exists as the Trinity, three persons, yet one.

Objects: At least three clover leaves

Can anyone tell me what kind of leaves these are? *(Hold up a few clover leaves so that all the children can see them, and pause for response.)* That's right, they're clover leaves. This *(hold up only one leaf)* is a clover leaf.

(Pick one leaflet from the stem and hold it so everyone can see it.) Is this a clover leaf? *(Pause for response. Be prepared for both yes and no.)* It's hard to tell, isn't it?

It looks like a whole leaf. There are no big holes in it. You can see where it attaches to the stem. *(Show the small stalk of the leaflet, then continue to hold the leaflet so that everyone can see it.)* But you know that it's really not the whole leaf, because I showed you the whole leaf. It's sort of a whole leaf, and sort of not, isn't it? We solve this problem by calling it a leaflet. This is a clover leaflet.

Yet, although we pulled it off the main stalk, it's still clover, isn't it? Would you call this dandelion? *(Pause for response.)* Or rose? Or daisy? Of course not! Even though it's a part of a full leaf, it's still clover. It's a clover leaflet.

(Hold up the stem with the remaining two leaflets.) Is this a clover leaf? *(Pause for response.)* Now you know the problem, don't you? This looks like more than a leaf. It looks like two leaves growing together. *(Show the stem.)* But it has one stem, so it's probably one leaf made of two leaflets. In fact, part of it is missing. *(Point out the space from the picked leaflet.)* So it isn't really a whole leaf. It's a leaf that we pulled apart. It's not complete; we need all three leaflets for a complete leaf.

(Continue to hold the leaf so that everyone can see it.) What kind of leaf is it? *(Pause for response.)* Yes, it's clover. It's not dandelion, or rose, or daisy. Although it's not a whole leaf, it's clover.

(Show another whole clover leaf.) Here's a whole clover leaf. You can always tell a clover leaf because of its three parts. All three parts are clover. Each leaflet is full and complete. *(Point out each leaflet.)* Yet, together the three make a clover leaf. *(Once more, the whole leaf.)*

That's the way it is with God. God is three parts, together making God. Yet each part is God, too. We call each part of God a person.

(Take one leaflet off the second clover leaf and hold it up.) It's like this one clover leaflet. We could call this Jesus. Is Jesus God? *(Pause for response.)* Yes! We know that Jesus is God the Son, that Jesus is a person who lived and died for our sins, yet he is God.

But there's more to God than just Jesus, isn't there? *(Hold up the rest of that clover leaf.)* To whom did Jesus pray? *(Pause for response.)* That's right! Jesus prayed to God the Father. Another part, or person, of God is the Father. *(Pick off another clover leaflet, and hold it up for all to see.)*

So we know that Jesus is God the Son *(hold up one clover leaflet)*, and there's also God the Father. *(Hold up the second leaflet.)*

Yet there's another part, or person, of God, isn't there? Can anyone tell me? *(Pause for response. If you have no response, say, "God the Father, God the Son, and God the_____" to have the children verbally fill in the blank.)* That's right, there's also God the Holy Spirit. *(Show the third clover leaflet.)* When Jesus went to heaven, he promised to send the Holy Spirit, didn't he? When people are baptized, they are baptized into the Father, the Son, and the Holy Spirit. *(Show each leaflet as you mention each person of the Trinity.)* Three persons, all God.

Yet, are there three Gods? *(Hold up one more complete clover leaf.)* No! There's only one. God said, "Behold, the Lord your God is one." Just like one clover leaf, God is one and only one God yet three persons—Father, Son, and Holy Spirit. *(Point out the three leaflets on one leaf.)* One leaf, three leaflets; one God, three persons.

We call God the Trinity. If you find that hard to understand, think of the clover—one leaf, three leaflets. And when you see a clover *(show a whole clover leaf)* you can think of God, three in one.

48

Don't Worry

Scripture: *And why do you worry about clothes? See how the lilies of the field grow. They do not labor or spin. Yet I tell you that not even Solomon in all his splendor was dressed like one of these. If that is how God clothes the grass of the field, which is here today and tomorrow is thrown into the fire, will he not much more clothe you, O you of little faith?* (Matt. 6:28–30).

Concept: God will take care of you.

Object: A large wildflower (or garden tiger lily), including the stem and some leaves. (Although this is done with a tiger lily, almost any wildflower will do. Pick out the tidbits that apply to your flower.)

See what I found this week! *(Show the flower.)* I picked it especially to show you how neat it is. God thought of everything this flower would need when he created it.

I brought a few of the leaves along, because the flower needs these leaves to bloom well. *(Point out the leaves.)* See how green they are? That means they work really well. Somehow, green leaves take sunshine and make it into plant food. When sunshine hits these leaves, tiny little "plant food factories" in the leaves swing into action and make food for the plant. We can't see it happen, and it's really complicated, but it works just right for the plant. I think that's really terrific.

The stem is another little wonder. *(Point out the stem.)* It looks like it's created to hold up the flower, doesn't it? It really does a whole lot more. Tiny tubes run from the bottom to the top of the stem, inside. *(Indicate where the tubes would run inside the stem.)* These tubes take water from the bottom of the plant and bring it up to the flower. They also take some minerals from the plant root and bring them up to the flower. They always bring just what the flower needs right up to it. How these tubes "know" what the flower needs is beyond me. I only know that they work just right for the flower.

Now look at the petals. *(Point out the petals.)* Aren't they gorgeous? Such a pretty orange. Not only are they pretty to us; some insects find them attractive, too. And this flower needs insects to help it make seeds. These petals attract just the right insects.

Can you smell this flower? *(Smell the flower yourself. Then whoosh it around them quickly.)* Maybe some of us can't, but the right kind of insects can. The insects that this flower needs are very sensitive to this flower's aroma. They can smell it a long way off, so they know exactly where to go.

176

See how broad the petals are? *(Indicate the wide petals. Some other flowers have specific landing platforms. Look for this ahead of time.)* That gives the insects plenty of room to land when they fly into the flower.

When an insect lands, it goes looking for nectar, a sweet juice that the flower makes. See these spots and streaks? *(Indicate the streaks on the petals.)* Where would an insect go if it followed the streaks? *(Walk your fingers down the streaks toward the center of the flower.)* That's right. It would go clear down to the center of the flower. That's right where the nectar is. And on the way, the insect picks up or drops off pollen. That's just what the plant needs to make seeds.

There are even some streaks that we can't see on flowers. Only certain insects can see them. That's the way they're created. But only certain insects need to see them for their own good and the good of the flowers.

Facts

Small individual flowers (hyacinths, goldenrod, lupine) often grow in bunches on a stalk to attract attention.

Night-blooming flowers (cereus, some cacti, yucca) are often heavily scented to attract pollinators.

Thorns and bristly leaves discourage large browsing animals.

Generally, low-lying flowers bloom before taller flowers, so each has its chance in the sun.

In composites (dandelions, daisies, asters) each petal is, botanically, a flower.

Flowers that rely on bees for pollination generally are not red. Bees cannot see red well.

Some very low-lying flowers (wild ginger) are pollinated by crawlers rather than fliers.

Continue Lesson

Can you see what I mean by how neat this flower is? God gave it everything that it needs to bloom and make seeds perfectly. I think that God put a lot of care into creating flowers.

Jesus once said that we should look at the flowers in a field to see how well they are made. He said that even King Solomon, with all his fine clothes, was not dressed as beautifully as God's flowers.

But Jesus didn't stop there. He went on to say that when we look at a flower and see how well it is made *(indicate the flower once more),* we should know that we never have to worry.

After all, God tells us that we're much more important to him than these flowers. If God takes such good care of flowers, and we're more important, won't he take care of us, too? *(Nod your head and pause for response.)* Of course he will! Jesus promised that. He said that we don't have to worry, because our heavenly Father knows exactly what we need.

So, we can take a lesson from this little flower and all the flowers that we see outside. We can see how beautiful they are and how well God cares for them. Then we can know that in God's eyes we are even more beautiful and that he will care for us.

49

Love, Love, Love!

Scripture: *A friend loves at all times* (Prov. 17:17).

"Love the Lord your God with all your heart and with all your soul and with all your mind and with all your strength." The second [most important commandment] is this: "Love your neighbor as yourself." There is no commandment greater than these (Mark 12:30–31).

For God so loved the world that he gave his one and only Son, that whoever believes in him shall not perish but have eternal life (John 3:16).

Dear friends, since God so loved us, we also ought to love one another (1 John 4:11).

And now these three remain: faith, hope and love. But the greatest of these is love (1 Cor. 13:13).

Concept: The best thing we can do is to show love.

Objects: Red hearts cut from construction paper with the above verses (or others of your choice) written on one side. If you want to read the verses in any special order, put little numbers on the hearts. A nice addition would be enough hearts so that each of the children can have one. Hand them out as the children return to their seats. (*Note:* This can be done in any season. Only the first paragraph refers to Valentine's Day. During any other season skip the first paragraph.)

Who can tell me what special day it will be this week? *(Pause for response.)* That's right, it's going to be Valentine's Day. There will be lots of hearts and flowers and talk about love this week.

(Hold up one of the hearts, with the printed side toward you.) What does this remind you of? *(Pause for response.)* That's right, it's a heart. It reminds us of love! People always use hearts to remind themselves of love.

This is going to be a very simple message, because I want to remind you of one very simple thing *(hold up the heart again):* love. The Bible says that love is very, very important. God loves us. God wants us to love him. The best thing that we can do in life is to love God and to love people.

Let me read to you just a few things that the Bible says about love. *(Read the verse from the back of the heart you are holding. Stress the word* love *and pause a second after you say it. Slowly put the heart down as you ask the next questions.)* A friend does what at all times? *(Tailor the question to the verse. Pause for response.)* Say it all together. *(Pause for response.)*

(Continue through the rest of the hearts this way. Read each one, stressing the word love. *Ask a question, based on the verse, which the children can answer with the word* love.*)*

Do you have the idea? The best thing that we can do for one another is to show *(pause for response)* love. God wants us to *(pause for response)* love him. And God *(pause for response)* loves us!

It's time to go back to your seats now. Every time you see one of these *(hold up a heart)* you'll think about *(pause for response)* that's right: love, love, love!

50

Death and New Life

Scripture: *Jesus said to her, "I am the resurrection and the life. He who believes in me will live, even though he dies; and whoever lives and believes in me will never die. Do you believe this?"* (John 11:25–26).

Concept: We have eternal life through Jesus.

Objects: Two bulbs (lily, amaryllis, crocus), one with a green shoot; a pot of soil. (Bulbs are available at nurseries. If one doesn't have a shoot, plant and water it well ahead of time to start its growth. If you do this during spring, you can add the option.)

(Show the children the bulb without a shoot.)

Can you see what I have here? It's a lily (or whatever) bulb. It looks quite dead, doesn't it? There's nothing growing from it. It's not making a plant or a flower. It's just a plain, "dead" bulb.

It may look dead to us. And if I keep it just like this, if I don't plant it, nothing will happen. It might as well be dead.

183

We can't see anything special about this bulb, can we? *(Shake your head and pause for response.)* But I know that if I plant this, it will "come back to life."

(Show the bulb with the shoot.) See this bulb? This was the same as the "dead" bulb. There was nothing to it. It would have stayed "dead." But someone planted it, and it sprang back to life. See the green shoot? *(Indicate the shoot.)* There's the life. That little shoot is going to grow into a big lily plant and it will probably even make a flower.

Option

If we look outside now, we can see lots of things springing to life. Grass, which looked dead all winter, is turning green with life. If you look closely in your garden or near your house, you may see some little shoots of plants that weren't there a few weeks ago. Everything seemed dead but now is returning to life.

Continue Lesson

Everything dies sometime, doesn't it? The lily that will come from this shoot won't live forever. It will turn brown and die. All the plants outside live for a little while and then die.

Even our pets will die. Do you know anyone who had a pet that died? *(Pause for response if you want the children to share a story.)*

Even people die, don't they? *(If you've had a death in the congregation lately, mention it.)* People get old, their bodies wear out, and they die. Sometimes people have accidents and they die. Someday, you and I will die, too.

But, do you know what? Jesus said that we won't be dead forever. Our bodies will die, just like the plant that grew from this bulb *(indicate the bulb without a shoot)* died. But the inside of us never has to die.

If we believe in Jesus, if we love him, he said that the inside of us will never die.

It's kind of like planting this bulb. *(Indicate the bulb without the shoot.)* If I plant this in good soil and take care of it *(plant the bulb in the pot as you speak)*, it will sprout again. It looks like it's dead now, but it will come back to life. *(Indicate the bulb with the shoot.)* That's what happened to this bulb.

And that's what will happen to us. If we're planted in Jesus *(indicate the pot with the planted bulb)*, we will not really die. Our lives will be new and different *(indicate the shoot on the bulb)*, but we will live.

All of our bodies will die someday. But if we believe in Jesus, we will never really die. We will always *(indicate the green shoot)* live in him.

Option

Spring is a good time to think about that. When you go outside and see everything turning green, you can think that there's new life outside. And you can remember that we will always have life if we believe in Jesus.

185

51

The Real Meaning of Christmas

> **Scripture**: *In him we have redemption through his blood, the forgiveness of sins, in accordance with the riches of God's grace that he lavished on us with all wisdom and understanding* (Eph. 1:7–8).
>
> **Concept**: Jesus was born to die for our sins.
>
> **Object**: A poinsettia plant

Can anyone tell me what kind of plant this is? (*Show the children the poinsettia plant. Pause for response.*) That's right, it's a poinsettia. We always see lots of them at Christmastime.

Have you ever wondered why we use poinsettias especially now? I have, so I looked it up. There are at least three reasons. I'm going to tell you one and help you guess at the other two.

First of all, a poinsettia is just a decoration. Poinsettias make pretty decorations, and we've used them around Christmastime for years. Now a poinsettia reminds us of Christmas. Using poinsettias is a pretty Christmas custom, that's all.

But, since we have a poinsettia here at Christmastime, we can use it to remind us of a whole lot more. Now, here's where you can help me.

Whose birthday do we celebrate at Christmas? *(Pause for response.)* That's right, we celebrate Jesus' birthday. That's not too hard to remember. We all see pictures of Baby Jesus and mangers and shepherds and all those things to remind us that Jesus was born. A poinsettia plant doesn't have to remind us of that, does it? Yet, some people say that the plant can help us remember *why* Jesus was born.

Look at all these green leaves. *(Indicate the leaves.)* People use lots of greenery around Christmas to remind them of life. Green plants are living things, and they can remind us of life that Jesus gave us. But that's not just this life, the life that our bodies have. This greenery reminds us of a better life than that. What kind of life did Jesus bring us? *(Pause for response. You may want to help by beginning to mouth "E.")* Yes! Jesus came into the world to bring us eternal life.

(Note: If all the children are very young, they won't understand "eternal." You can end the preceding paragraph at the reminder of life that Jesus gave us. Then simply say "eternal" in the next paragraph.)

So at Christmastime we can look at the green leaves of this plant and remember the eternal life that Jesus brought us.

Even these red flowers can remind us of something. *(Note: The red "flowers" are really bracts. True poinsettia flowers are the little things at the center of the bracts. Depending on how correct you want to be, you could say "bracts" or "red leaves.")* What did Jesus have to do to give us eternal life? What did he do near the end of his life? He not only lived for us, but he also *(pause for response)* died for us. Jesus died on the cross so that we could have eternal life.

Now, what does this red remind you of? *(Pause for response.)* It does look like splashes of blood, doesn't it? That's what a lot of people say. The red in a poinsettia can remind you of Jesus' blood, which he shed for us when he was a grown man.

So, every time you see a poinsettia around Christmastime, you can think of three things. First, the whole plant *(indicate the whole plant)* can remind you that who was born? *(Pause for response.)* Yes! It reminds you that Jesus was born. The splashes of red *(indicate the red bracts)* remind you of Jesus' *(pause for response)* blood that he shed for us. And the green leaves *(indicate the leaves)* remind us of *(pause for response)* the eternal life that Jesus gives us.

I think a poinsettia *(indicate the whole plant)* is a really nice plant to have around at Christmastime, don't you?

52

A Fruit Bowl of Christians

Scripture: *There is neither Jew nor Greek, slave nor free, male nor female, for you are all one in Christ Jesus* (Gal. 3:28).

Concept: We are all equal in Christ.

Object: A bowl with different kinds of fruit in it

Here's one of my favorite things. *(Show the bowl of fruit.)* A bowl filled with fruit! If I want a snack, all I have to do is dip into this fruit bowl. *(Set the bowl in front of you and pick out one fruit.)*

(Hold up the fruit for the children to see.) Here's an apple! How many of you like apples? *(Pause for response.)* I do, too. You don't even have to peel an apple before you eat it. Even the skin is good for you, if the apple is washed. Some of you may not like apples, but we all know that they are good fruits.

(Put the apple back and hold up another fruit.) An orange! Who likes oranges? *(Pause for response.)* Lots of people—maybe not everyone, but lots of people— like oranges. You can peel them or just cut them open. You can make orange juice, or eat the juicy

189

fruit just the way it is. Oranges have lots of vitamin C; they're good fruits, too.

(Continue in this manner until you've run out of fruit or nearly out of time. Mention something good about each fruit; acknowledge the fact that maybe some people don't like it, but it is a fruit and it is good.)

Each of these fruits is good in some way. There's really not one better than the other, is there? We may like some more than others, because we have different tastes. The fruits are different, but they're all good for us. They're all fruits.

That's why we call this bowl a fruit bowl. We don't call it an apple-orange-banana bowl. When we look at the whole thing, we say, "There's fruit."

God looks at all of us in much the same way. He can look at all of us sitting together here and say, "There are my children."

Of course, God knows each one of us. Just as we look at this bowl *(indicate the bowl and the fruits as you speak)* and say, "There's an apple, an orange, and a banana," God can look at us and say, "There's Kendra, Zach, and Tanner." *(Use names of children present.)*

And God loves each one of us separately, just as we love each fruit. God will say, "I love Matthew. I love Meggy. I love Emily," just as we might say, "I love oranges, I love apples, I love bananas." *(Indicate each fruit as you speak.)*

But there's a little difference. We love the fruits because we like the way they taste. Maybe we don't love all fruits. But God loves us all the same, because we are all his children. The Bible tells us that we are all one, we are all equal, in Jesus. God loves each one of us as much as he loves the next one. To God, we are all equal. Each of us is his child.

So, the next time you see a bowl full of fruit *(indicate the bowl)* you can think of us sitting right here. And you can remember that God looks at us and sees us all as his children.

And if you're tempted to eat all of the apples but leave the oranges *(indicate one kind)*, you can think of God who loves us all equally. Each one of us is his favorite child.